✳ Fiction ✳

Contents

PAGE 114

PAGE 146

PAGE 166

✳ Features ✳

✳ Fancy That! ✳

PAGE 18

PAGE 6

PAGE 163

✳ Teatime Treats ✳

PAGE 81

PAGE 157

DC Thomson

While every reasonable care will be taken, neither D C Thomson & Co, Ltd, nor its agents accept liability for loss or damage to any material submitted to this publication.

COVER PICTURE: DAVID VENNI/CELEBRITY PICTURES INSIDE COVER DESIGN: MANDY MURRAY

Make Time For YOU!

Me-time is essential for body and spirit – and like these busy celebrities, it's all about enjoying life's little pleasures…

Mountain High

Kate's a highly-accomplished skier – and it's rumoured that she's even better than William!

The happy couple enjoyed regular skiing trips before they married but skipped their annual Alpine break last winter. However, as the Queen's holiday home in the Scottish Highlands is near several ski centres, Kate can always head to the slopes during visits to her in-laws at Balmoral Castle!

Just Relax

When Holly needs to escape from the stresses and strains of being a working mum with two little girls, she doesn't need to travel far to find sanctuary. "The bath is my answer to most things," said Holly. "There's nothing better than a soak with some candles and a book."

On The Beach

Lorraine makes the most of her precious me-time by taking her dog, Rocky, for a walk whenever she has a free moment.

"I love walking my dog," said Lorraine, who lives in Dundee, on the east coast of Scotland, with her husband Steve, daughter Rosie and Rocky. "We live very close to the beach and go for big, long walks."

In fact, walking is one of Lorraine's favourite modes of transport. "I'm a huge advocate of walking," continued Lorraine. "I've always got a pair of flat shoes in my handbag."

FACT!
As well as blowing cobwebs away, sea breezes are packed full of health-boosting particles of energy

More Overleaf

Puppy Love

When Miranda's in need of some "me-time", she leaves behind her London home to spend a weekend in an isolated, very remote seaside cottage. "I love being on my own," said Miranda, who's accompanied on her regular escapes to the coast by her Shi Tzu cross, Peggy. "There's nobody else there, although I chat to Peggy like a mad eccentric!"

FACT!
Research shows that talking to pets about problems and worries is good for your health

Fine Dining

"Going out for dinner is my favourite thing in the whole world," said TV presenter Christine Bleakley, who revealed that she doesn't care where she goes, just as long as the food's good!

"It could be the local Chinese restaurant or some fancy place or anything in between," she continued. "I just love that whole experience.

"If I have a hobby, it's eating out."

Pampered!

Comedienne, actress and scriptwriter Ruth Jones finds it impossible to resist beauty treatments, preferably somewhere luxurious! "I'm a bit of a spa addict. I could happily be pampered all day with facials and massages."

Since losing weight last year, Ruth has discovered another indulgence! "I used to hate going clothes shopping," said Ruth, who admitted that, now she's slimmer, shopping has become a lot more enjoyable!

At Home

"What makes me happy are the simplest things," revealed Dawn, who lists "pottering about at my home in Cornwall" as one of her favourite pastimes.

Dawn's another celebrity who enjoys taking her dog for a walk, with twice-daily jaunts across the Cornish countryside. "Life is good," said a contented Dawn.

WORDS: WENDY GLASS   PICTURES: GETTY IMAGES, PRESS ASSOCIATION, ALAMY, ALPHA PRESS, KAREN ROBINSON/THE GUARDIAN, THINKSTOCK, REX FEATURES

By best-selling novelist

Wendy Holden

Lady Of The House

It's not all a life of leisure for nobility; this lady feels the pressure of entertaining royal guests in her stately home

The visitors would be here soon. I made one slow, final tour round the Great Salon with its silken sofas and flicked invisible dust from the Louis XVI sidetables bearing silk-framed photographs of royalty. Those of the throne's current occupants, the ones we expected today, I made sure were in the most prominent positions.

Satisfied at last, I glanced up at the gilt-framed portraits staring down from the wall. There was, I felt, approval in their eyes. The latest generation of the family, they seemed to be saying, was making a decent fist of keeping things up.

As I passed beneath it, the enormous

There was a particular one called Susan who had actually looked me in the eye recently, and another, Helen, who had so far forgotten herself as to ask me a direct question. No doubt it was her mother's fault. Calling one's daughter after a legendary mythical beauty and queen was obviously incompatible with the lifetime of domestic service which Helen and her like could expect. I had told Peach to rename her Ruby. That would put her in her place.

Standing, now, at the enormous plate-glass window with its view over the Long Water and the magnificent parkland, I admired the great flat sweep

The newer girls seemed less respectful than was ideal for their station in life

central chandelier sparkled in the late morning light, its turning facets throwing a shower of brilliant colours over the polished parquet and panelled walls.

I was glad to see that Mrs Peach, the housekeeper, and her army of servants had been as hard at work as ever. A relief, as some of the newer girls seemed less respectful than was ideal.

of uninterrupted green galloping away to the curved horizon. We were truly fortunate in having Cudlipp as head gardener, despite the efforts of Her Majesty, on her last visit, to persuade him down to Windsor.

I shook my head – carefully so as not to dislodge the hat – and pondered on what **Continued overleaf…**

ILLUSTRATIONS: MANDY MURRAY, THINKSTOCK

All was ready for the distinguished visitors

Continued from previous page

what my nearest aristocratic neighbour, Countess Haddon, had recently confided about Queen Mary's visit there. She had taken a fancy to some chased silver cruets on the dining table, and of course, once she had admired something, one was obliged to make her Majesty a present of it.

"Lock up your best silver, my dear Cynthia," Margaret Haddon had advised me. I had followed her counsel to the letter – only the second-best Sèvres for dinner tonight – and instructed Cudlipp to keep out of the way.

I wandered through into the dining room with its great coffered gold and white ceiling. The table stretched away from me like a brown and polished lake, but not for long, I knew. Soon, Henderson the butler and his footmen would be marching in to set it for lunch. Everything was ready; the menu had been decided

second footman was discovered to have been intercepting the champagne. He was last seen, so I am told, lying in the street outside the village hostelry, having also intercepted a great deal of gin.

I saw, through the enfilade of doors at the end of the room, a full figure like Mrs Peach's bustle past, although rather too swiftly for me, in my day dress stiff with pearls and embroidery, to call her. I wasn't in the habit of shrieking after servants and preferred to pull the bell by the fireplace. But pull it I would; I wanted to be sure, from the housekeeper's own lips, that the bedrooms upstairs were prepared and every eventuality anticipated. Royalty was notoriously demanding, and in more than one way in this case of course.

The Queen had been given the second best State bedroom, the Duke and myself having decided that the best was simply

I wanted to be sure all was ready for our guests, every eventuality anticipated

on weeks ago. Consommé, fish, venison and rarebit. The river-keeper had supplied some fine fat trout and the deer, from the park herd, had hung in the game larder some days. Cudlipp had delivered to the kitchen back door an impressive selection of garden vegetables.

Henderson had been down to the vast cellars and selected the wine, which would hopefully survive until the required moment. We wanted no repeat of the unfortunate business when the Bourbon-Parmas had stayed and the

too much of a risk. The pictures there could not be removed, and they included Titians and Caravaggios. The second best bedroom had some attractive but essentially worthless pastoral oils, to which the Queen was welcome. However, we had quietly put away the Charles I dressing-table set with the solid silver mirror.

His Majesty would of course not notice the paintings in the best bedroom, stamps being the focus of his interest. Stamps and punctuality. Dick Dent, the

The King would be admiring our horses

clock-winder, had been at work for days making sure every timepiece in the house was on Sandringham Time, the King's own special time which was half an hour ahead of Greenwich. This had led to a great deal of confusion during the middle part of the week when people were uncertain which time was right. The Duke and I had endured a wait of half an hour for the cheese course on one occasion, and on another had been inconvenienced by baths prepared half an hour too early and gone cold.
Continued overleaf…

Continued from previous page

The visitors seemed late, I thought, but it always took some time, in a house of this huge size, to reach the salon. No doubt they had been waylaid at the stables, home to my husband's new favourite toy. Sinbad, the new Arab stallion, was by all accounts settling in happily, as indeed he should, our stables being among the most magnificent of any country house in England.

An interest in bloodstock had always been a tradition in our family and I knew it was said – and with truth – that the horses had better accommodation and food than anyone in the surrounding villages.

The King would be admiring the horses, and possibly choosing a mount of his own to ride in the next few days. That His Majesty would expect outdoor diversions had been the focus of my husband's preparation. It was the shooting season, a sport on which the monarch was especially keen.

Armies of beaters had been engaged, and extra waiting staff to take the great hampers up and serve lunch on the moors – white gloves, silver and all. Carefully-chosen guns had been invited and the moors made ready. Thousands of pheasants were now striding around the heather quite unperturbed, unaware that the next few days were destined to be their last.

I could hear voices in the distance now and, for all my calm preparation, was unable to prevent a sudden thrill of terror. For all our family was one of the foremost in the land, to be visited by royalty remained the highest of honours.

As the hostess I felt the responsibility particularly keenly. I was co-ordinator of the festivities, focus and facilitator of all that had been planned and decided on. It all began and ended with me; praise if it went well, blame if it didn't.

Everything was ready, but one could never, in these situations, rule out the possibility of some unexpected oversight, some unforeseen disaster. Which, if it happened, would transmit itself faster than Sinbad himself to the gloating ears of Margaret Haddon and her like. We great aristocrats and society hostesses were immaculately polite to each other on all occasions, but none of us ever doubted that we were rivals.

Nervously I fingered the diamonds around my neck and checked my reflection in the gilt-framed mirror over the carved marble fireplace. My face stared back, steady-eyed, straight-nosed, level-chinned, unimpeachably patrician and, thank goodness, topped by a straight tiara. Elsie, my newest lady's maid, had much steadier hands than Gladys, her predecessor, but of course there had been a reason for that; one not unconnected with the second footman's intercepting activities.

The voices were drawing nearer; they seemed to have reached the Blue Salon, which was the first of the house's long sequence of drawing rooms. They would have to pass through the Pink Salon and then the Gold before reaching me in the Great Salon, our traditional receiving room for distinguished visitors, in the heart of the house.

Elsie, I now realised, had laced me up unwontedly tightly. How else to explain the constriction of chest I now felt? I could hardly breathe all of a sudden, and my face felt burning hot.

My heart, confined in this cage of whalebone and laces, was banging with painful violence. I clutched the back of a chair with one hand and pressed the back of the other wrist to the top of a nearby marble table to cool it.

"And this is the Gold Salon," I heard a voice say on the other side of the doors.

My heart seemed to be forcing itself into my throat and there was terrible pain in my head. I stared up at the painted ceiling and felt as if Mars, up there with his red cloak and his great sword, had plunged it through my brow. I tried to breathe but could not.

My eyes, straining and panic-stricken, locked themselves on the ornate golden handles of the double Great Salon doors, which were now twisting and opening.

I stepped forward in my heavy dress. "Your Majesties!" I managed to cry out through my thick throat, before crashing heavily to the Gobelins carpet, where I lay, conscious but utterly unable to move.

There was an astonished silence, then the muffled thud of nearing footsteps on thick rug.

"Bloody hell, look! It's Cynthia!" said someone. "She's fainted."

"Ring the ambulance, Helen, she looks as if she's having some kind of fit."

"I've told her she was taking on too many hours. It's only volunteering, after all. She doesn't have to steward the rooms every single day."

"I know, Sue, but she's completely obsessed with the place. And she's no family, nothing else to do. Honestly, I sometimes wonder if she doesn't sort of fancy herself as living here… in the old days, sort of thing…"

As hostess I felt the responsibility keenly; success all began and ended with me

"You know she told Helen she was going to call her Ruby from now on, don't you?" said another voice incredulously. "Because it was more suitable for an under-parlourmaid."

"She never!"

"She did, too," came the reply. "Too much *Downton Abbey*, that's what I reckon. Look, is that ambulance coming or what? The first bus tour'll be here in a sec. We shoved them into the shops in the stable block as long as we could, but they'll be coming for a look-round any minute now…"

Turn the page for more from Wendy…

Wendy Holden

Edwardian Chic

The best-selling author explains to us her fascination with laced-up period finery…

As a child I often imagined myself in the black stockings and sailor suits worn by *The Railway Children*, while that narrow-hipped-skirt-and-full-bloused Gibson Girl look captivated me as a teenager. I've always been drawn to the clothes of the Edwardian era. It seemed so feminine and romantic, and at the same time quite sporty and tidy. I especially loved the jolly ties some women wore with their full-sleeved white blouses when playing tennis in straw boaters.

My absolute favourite Edwardian ladies were royals – Queen Mary with her impenetrable lace embonpoint was the epitome of stern elegance, while Queen Alexandra with her bustles and big, wistful eyes was the last word in glamour. Of course, achieving the look was a nightmare, the engineering beneath the clothes was worthy of Isambard Kingdom Brunel and the materials were often thick and hot. The obligation for Edwardian aristocracy to change clothes a hundred times a day – for breakfast, lunch, tea and dinner – cannot have made life easy either. But the knowledge that these clothes were basically a tyranny doesn't make them any less fascinating.

The most wonderful Edwardian outfit I can think of is the dress preserved at Kedleston Hall, near

Queen Mary

Queen Alexandra

I'm hugely relieved not to have to wear, or wash, such labour-intensive outfits

where I live in Derbyshire, which Lady Curzon wore in the early 1900s while Vicereine of India. It has peacocks and jewels embroidered all over it and glitters, even now, like a firework display. What it must have been like to wear it under the broiling Indian sun hardly bears thinking about, but no doubt Lady Curzon laced up and thought of England.

While I'm hugely relieved not to have to wear such labour-intensive outfits and even more relieved not to be obliged to wash and iron them, there is a delicacy and beauty to the Edwardian look which seems to speak to everyone. Especially the lovely evening wear. There's something heavenly about the sweeping skirts and the huge plumed hats under which the plainest face looked intriguing. Edwardian femininity was about concealment, and in our over-exposed, too-tight, muffin-topped and fake-tanned age, the idea of an era where even flashing an ankle was risqué seems too delicious for words.

Turn the page to *Downton Abbey*

PICTURES: REX FEATURES, ALAMY, GETTY IMAGES

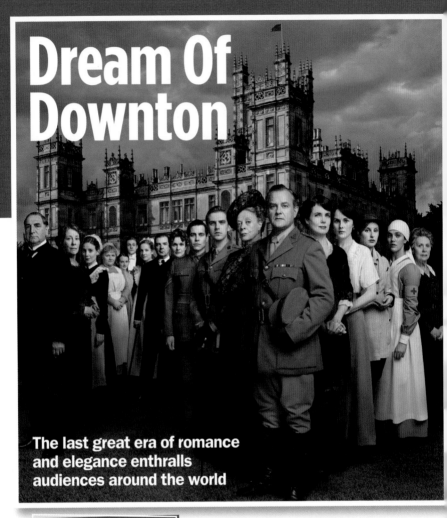

Dream Of Downton

The last great era of romance and elegance enthralls audiences around the world

The Real World

Behind the affluence of Downton is a world where the wanton waste of life in the trenches was followed by the ravages of a flu pandemic – all in an era of flapper girls!

The Edwardian era's strict hierarchy of masters and servants and corseted emotions is a perennial favourite with TV audiences. From the pent-up passions behind Lady Mary and Matthew Crawley's romance, and the indomitable figure of the Dowager Duchess, to the turmoil behind the uniforms in the Servants Hall, the fortunes and dramas are avidly followed. Even the classless society of the USA has taken to the classy soap, with Shirley MacLaine joining the cast, and looking set to challenge Dame Maggie Smith for acting awards and prizes in the stiff-upper-lip-belies-a-heart-of-gold stakes.

Who's A Lovely Boy?

Generous Dan's the kind of man to follow his heart – but will it ever lead him to more than just job satisfaction?

By Della Galton

an glanced at his watch as he parked outside the vet's. He hoped they wouldn't keep him too long – he was supposed to be at work, but Grace had been so upset when he'd seen her this morning that he'd found himself impulsively offering to help.

He hadn't meant right at that moment, but his neighbour was a little deaf. So, not wanting to disappoint her, he'd loaded Monty's cage into the back of his van. Well, he could hardly let Grace take him to the vet's on the bus, which was what

people in the waiting room – just a man with a nervous-looking collie and an elderly lady with a giant ginger cat which yowled loudly from its carry-basket.

Their owners smiled at him and he smiled back with a brightness he didn't feel. Hopefully his boss wouldn't mind him being a bit late as long as he made up the time later.

"Oh dear, he doesn't look too happy, does he?" The pretty vet, who introduced herself as Kate, nodded sympathetically as Dan set the cage gently on the table and explained that Grace was worried about her beloved bird.

Faced with those gorgeous blue eyes, it wasn't just the parrot who'd gone quiet

she'd been planning – could he?

"Here we are then, mate." He lifted the large domed cage carefully out of the van. "Let's go and see what's wrong with you, shall we?"

The red and grey parrot was hunched over his perch. Dan didn't know a thing about parrots but he had to admit that Monty looked pretty sorry for himself.

To his relief, there weren't many

"Is he off his food at all?"

"Er – yes, and he's very quiet," Dan stuttered. He seemed to have lost his voice all of a sudden too. It must be the effect of those gorgeous blue eyes that were studying him with interest.

"I'll check his temperature," she said.

"Right." He was feeling a little overheated himself. His heart rate must be sky-high too.

"I think he has an infection," Kate said, as she finished her examination. "So I'm going to give him some antibiotics, which should clear it up quite quickly. I'll need to see him again in about a week. Are you a relative – are you able to bring him in?"

"No, I'm just a neighbour," Dan explained. "But yes, I can bring him – no problem. Grace will be thrilled that it's not serious. She adores him."

Kate smiled. "She's very lucky to have you. Pets are a lifeline for lots of elderly people, but getting them to the vet's can be a problem. It was lovely of you to bring him."

Continued overleaf…

"It's no problem," he said, feeling himself melt a little more.

He was brought swiftly down to earth by a text from his boss, just as he was putting the cage carefully back into the van. *You're supposed to be in a meeting! Where are you?*

He cursed. He'd forgotten all about the meeting, which was to discuss the future of the company. Oops! Still – telling a delighted Grace that Monty was going to be absolutely fine would be worth the ticking off he'd get. And meeting the delectable Kate had been a bonus too!

So what happened at the meeting?" Dan asked Janice when he collected his deliveries from the stores.

lose their job, these days.

Over the next few weeks Dan did his best to stick to the new regime but he really missed his chats with the customers. He felt as though he was on an endless treadmill.

By the end of the month he'd had enough. He'd more or less decided to hand in his notice – although what else he was going to do for a living he didn't know. Fortunately, he'd got some savings put by, so he wouldn't have to make an instant decision.

He'd just got in from work the following evening when Grace came out of her front door.

"Dan, dear, I don't suppose you'd do me an enormous favour, would you?"

"It's a shame. I think part of the job is making sure the customer's happy"

"More or less what we were expecting," she murmured, shaking her head. "They've set even higher targets and they're introducing a 'driver of the month' bonus, although if you actually managed to cram in all the deliveries they're expecting, you'd be exhausted.

"Talking to customers is discouraged – apart from getting them to sign for deliveries." Janice smiled ruefully. "Why waste time talking when you can be driving, eh?"

"It's a shame," Dan agreed. "I personally think part of the job is making sure the customer's happy."

"None of the drivers are happy, that's for sure. A few were muttering about looking for other jobs, but I expect they'll settle down again in a couple of weeks."

Dan nodded, sure she was right. After all, not many people could afford to

"Yes, of course – it's not Monty again, is it?" he said in alarm. The parrot had been fine when he'd taken him back for his check-up.

"Monty's grand, thank you, dear. No, it's my friend, Sylvia at number twenty-three. Her Alfie – that's her cat – is a bit off colour, and I was wondering if you might give her a lift to that nice vet's who got my Monty right?"

And so on Saturday he found himself standing in front of Kate again, this time, in charge of one very fluffy black cat.

"Fur balls," she pronounced, having examined a spitting and unco-operative Alfie. "Is he always this unfriendly?"

"He's not mine," Dan confessed. "He belongs to another of my elderly neighbours – she's just had a hip replacement and can't get out."

Kate looked at him thoughtfully. "Well,

it's very good of you to bring him – we used to have a collection and delivery service attached to the practice, but Jim, the driver, retired recently and we haven't replaced him yet."

"Are you planning to replace him?" Dan asked, a flicker of excitement beginning in his stomach.

"Well, yes, we'd like to – but there aren't many drivers around who can cope with sick animals, not to mention anxious owners." She smiled at him. "Why? Do you know anyone that might be interested?"

"Yes, I think I might," Dan murmured.

When he gave in his notice his boss sighed and wished him well. "I'll be sorry to see you go, Dan, you're one of our best drivers. You could do very well under the new system – in your pay packet, I mean, where it counts."

"It's just a pity it's at the expense of customer service and job satisfaction," Dan said as they shook hands.

Money wasn't everything. He knew that better than anyone. It wasn't the first time he'd given up a job when he'd stopped enjoying it. But he had a feeling that it might be the last.

A month later, on a beautiful spring afternoon, he drove Iris and her spaniel, Max, back home from the vet's.

"Thanks, love. It was such a relief to find Max only has a virus." Iris touched
Continued overleaf…

Continued from previous page

his arm as they walked up to her front door along a path lined with sunshine-yellow daffodils. "I don't suppose you'd like a coffee and a slice of my home-made Madeira? Perhaps you haven't got time?"

"I've always time for a quick cuppa, thank you very much."

Her face lit up. Dan smiled and thought that his old boss had been wrong. No amount of extra money could make up for the satisfaction of a job well done. Seeing the pleasure in

passionately, the previous night. "Not spread sheets and computers."

He was whistling as he arrived back at the surgery for his last pick-up. Kate was finishing some paperwork at the reception desk. She glanced up and her eyes warmed.

"Hi, Dan, I'll fetch Spot. He's been so patient."

"Before you do, Kate –" He broke off, suddenly shy. How was it that he could chat until the cows came home about day-to-day stuff, but when he had something important to say, all his words died in his throat?

Why was it he could chat all day – until he had something important to say?

Iris's eyes as she looked at her beloved dog – and hearing the smile in her voice as she told him how she'd raised him from a tiny pup – now what could be more rewarding than that?

Fortunately, Kate had a completely different attitude towards work. She'd built up her small practice from scratch and she really cared about her patients.

Kate was a delight. Naturally reserved, she was more relaxed around animals than people. But over the last few weeks they'd chatted more and more. He knew she'd once had a disastrous relationship with a vet who'd cheated on her and now she found it difficult to trust.

She knew he'd once qualified as an accountant but had found no fulfilment in days spent with numbers not people.

"Life's about people," he'd told her

"Before I do…?" Kate chewed the end of her pen and looked at him expectantly.

"I was wondering if – we – well, if you would like…"

"Yes…?"

She smiled and, encouraged, he went on quickly. "To have dinner one evening – with me?"

Kate's gorgeous blue eyes sparkled. "I thought you'd never ask," she said.

A WORD FROM THE AUTHOR

"Having three dogs, I spend a fair bit of time at the vet's and the waiting room is a fascinating place to be. A young man bringing in his neighbour's parrot for a check-up inspired this story."

ILLUSTRATIONS: JAMES DEWAR, THINKSTOCK

Fancy That!

Easter facts that make you go "**Wow**!"

■ Easter comes from Eostre, goddess of spring, who is symbolised by the hare and egg.

■ **The Easter egg hunt on the White House lawn has been a tradition since 1878.**

Pysanka is the practice of Easter egg painting

The season begins on Easter Day for 50 days, ending at Pentecost

■ **Easter falls on the first Sunday after the full moon after March 21. If the full moon falls on Sunday, Easter is the next Sunday.**

■ The eleven balls of marzipan around a Simnel cake represent the disciples, excluding Judas.

■ **Easter Island, 2180 miles west of Chile is a tiny 63sq miles, with no permanent source of fresh water.**

Each year nearly 90 million chocolate bunnies are made

■ The custom of giving eggs goes back to ancient Egyptians, for whom it was a symbol of life.

■ **The Easter bunny is popular in the UK and US, but in Australia they use their native marsupial, the Bilby.**

■ **Some think a hot cross bun represents the crucifix, but loaves with crosses were eaten by Saxons, to symbolise the four quarters of the moon.**

■ The largest chocolate Easter egg was 25ft high and weighed 8968lbs.

Easter Bonnets go back to when people denied themselves wearing of their finery during Lent

The first Easter baskets were made to look like birds' nests

Music In The Hills

The beautiful Austrian scenery and fresh mountain air give Carol much-needed time to think about her future…

By Lydia Jones

D o you remember the words of that song from *The Sound Of Music* about being sixteen going on seventeen and all that goes with it?

Didn't you just want to be Liesl Von Trapp: twirling around an Austrian summerhouse and looking radiantly beautiful in a flouncy skirt?

I know I did. I danced along park benches pretending I was really the daughter of a rich Austrian Count.

That film made me want to come here. With my youthful world-is-waiting-to-be-explored optimism, I imagined snow capped mountains and spring green figure who has difficulty deciding what to wear each morning? At least that's one advantage of a walking holiday: no need to dress up.

"Mind if I join you?"

He has an open face and a smile that creases tanned skin at his temples in an endearing way. I notice well-worn walking boots and matching blue socks.

Previously he's been at the front of our group: a collection of strangers on a "guided walking tour of the Austrian Tirol". My daughter signed me up.

"It'll do you good, Mum – give you space to think."

She's a social worker who spends her working life doing her best to sort out people's problems.

My daughter spends her life sorting out problems – I'm sorry to have become one

meadows. And half a century later, here they are.

My twirling days are long gone. Stumbling is more my style now; has been ever since I lost Ian.

I brought up three children and ran a house single-handed while my husband was frequently away for business.

How did I become this shambolic

I am sorry to have somehow become one of them.

"I'm Geoff," says Mr Matching Socks. "Carol."

We exchange usual introductory information and comment on scenery. It's not challenging stuff but still my stomach fizzes like soluble aspirin. When **Continued overleaf…**

I've always
wanted to
do this

Gentians nestle in the meadow

Continued from previous page
you've been half of a couple for almost forty years you lose the knack of talking to men. Especially attractive ones.

"Oh!" A field of cobalt blue steals my breath with wonder.

"Gentians," Geoff says. "Nursery-grown ones aren't a patch on the real deal, are they?"

We stop to soak in their beauty; Geoff breaks open a bar of chocolate. We munch in companionable silence. It's sort of comfortable – or it would be, if I could shake off the guilt at being with anyone other than Ian like this.

At the lunch stop Sue is marshalling her team of ladies. We've only been here a couple of days but already she is

"We're all agreed, dear."

There is a general murmur of assent.

I'm peeved: according to the prospectus, this afternoon offers the best possibility of finding the elusive Edelweiss. Ever since Christopher Plummer picked up his guitar to sing about them, I have wanted to see one.

"Okay. How many are we?" Sue stands, brushing crumbs from her jeans. Her counting finger pauses at me.

"Actually," Geoff says, "Carol and I are walking together this afternoon."

My head swivels as if pulled by a string; Geoff grins. In side-vision I see Sue's mouth forming an "O".

I blush and beam him a look of gratitude for rescuing me from bossy-boots Sue.

I'm sort of comfortable with Geoff, or I would be if I could shake off the guilt

the self-appointed organiser of the single female contingent.

"Poor Amanda has twisted her ankle," she says, taking a large bite of a ham and smoked cheese sandwich. "It's probably best we all head back in the hotel minibus."

"No, really –" Amanda squeaks.

It's wonderful. We take stepping stones over crystal streams; cross wooden bridges with little roofs.

Along the way, Geoff points out plants to me; snow-kissed peaks glitter like gems in sunshine. And right near the end, we get our reward, a meadow white-star splashed with Edelweiss.

"See," I want to say to Ian. "It's a real flower – not just something made up for the film, like you said."

But he isn't with me. Never will be again. So I content myself with staring while in a skin-pricklingly surreal moment Geoff squeezes my hand.

Tonight it's a Folklore Evening. Through silver twilight, in horse-drawn carts, we ascend twisting mountain roads lined by pillars of pine.

Irritation flashes as visions of my solitary lake-side drink vanish.

Decision time, Carol: please the "girls" or please Geoff?

Then, suddenly, it hits me; there is someone else I can please.

Someone whose needs I have often neglected.

"Actually I'm planning on taking the train to Zell-Am-See."

"On your own?"

Sue's jaw drops and Geoff looks hurt. I'm sorry for that, but tempting as it is to

It suddenly hits me – there is someone whose needs I have often neglected

The silence is eerie and without thinking I find myself leaning into Geoff, with whom I have somehow managed to be sharing a seat.

He finds us a table; goes to get drinks and I remember all the lovely things about being a couple. Between glasses of chilled white wine I exhale recent tensions and enjoy the sensation of Geoff taking charge.

"Free day tomorrow. The girls are going to Vipetino duty-free shopping. Coming, Carol?" Sue eyes me with the cautious disappointment she has conveyed ever since Geoff and I began walking together.

"Err –"

I had sort of thought about sampling some of that space my daughter recommended: taking a train to Zell-Am-See; I'd imagined myself sitting beside the lake, alone, sipping hot chocolate.

"Carol and I are visiting Mad King Ludwig's Castle," Geoff pipes up before I can speak. "Bit of a journey, but worth it."

Are we? Did we discuss this?

surrender, I'm not ready for him or anybody else to tell me what to do right now.

Maybe I never will be again.

And here, beside Zell's glittering lake, another *Sound Of Music* song comes to mind; this one all about being confident, in both the world around us and in ourselves.

Well, maybe I am a little bit. At least it's coming back.

My husband may have decided to dispense with our marriage, but sipping a tasty hot chocolate in this beautiful place, I realise at last that my life is far from over.

In fact it's just beginning.

A WORD FROM THE AUTHOR
"Austria is a place close to my heart, as I have spent many happy holidays there. And although it is deeply unfashionable, I absolutely love *The Sound Of Music*!"

A Little Bird Told Me

Everyone should have a special place to feel safe and secure, a comfortable nest they can call their own…

By Jane Sevenoaks

There's a bird in your shed." Ruth dropped her trowel and looked round quickly, her heart thumping out of her chest.

"Edward, you startled me."

Her seven-year-old neighbour was looking at her anxiously.

"There's a blackbird in your shed," he repeated, his eyes fixed on the open shed door. "I saw it picking up bits of twig so I followed it."

Ruth got up off her knees with some difficulty and went to the open door of the shed. There was indeed a nest. Her heart sank.

"But…"

"For at least a fortnight. Actually, no, a month." Her husband was trying, she realised, to suppress a happy smile.

"It's a good shed, and there's an awful lot of stuff in it," he began, but stopped short at her stern look.

"There's a nest," she said, "perched between the handles of your garden shears. Four eggs. You'll have to wait for them to fledge."

"That's fine," her husband said happily.

"And you can't go in," she admonished. "You'll disturb her."

"But I need…"

"You'll just have to wait," she said, shrugging. "And you'll have to leave the door open."

"I thought you said the-sooner-the-better, that no-man-needs-two-sheds"

"You can't get rid of the shed," Ruth said regretfully to George, her husband, that evening as they were washing up the dishes. "Well, not yet anyway."

George put down the plate he was drying. "I thought you said the-sooner-the-better. I thought you said no-man-needs-two-sheds, I thought you said…"

"I know what I said," his wife replied wearily, "but you'll have to put it off."

"I can't! There's my axe in there, and a ladder, and goodness knows what else. We'll be murdered in our beds!"

His wife snorted. The subject was definitely closed.

You know," her husband said a few days later as he came into the kitchen for a cup of coffee, "now that I'm using the other shed more, I realise how

ILLUSTRATIONS: KIRK HOUSTON, THINKSTOCK

The blackbird had made herself at home

good it is. It's more like a summerhouse."

"Plenty of room for all your stuff."

"Maybe I should replace the odd floorboard." They both stood looking out at the dilapidated building. "I built that shed from scratch," George continued. "It's got electricity and everything. Maybe I could put a chair in it. You could

sit out there with a nice cup of tea."

He drained his cup and headed back outside, oblivious to his wife's incredulous look.

George spent the next few days going in and out of the summerhouse (as he now called it), sawing, hammering and **Continued overleaf…**

Continued from previous page

painting, and often accompanied by Edward, who would furtively inspect the nest.

The following week George announced that he had finished. Ruth made some tea and followed George and Edward out to the summerhouse. It was surprisingly light and airy in there, and really quite warm, out of the wind.

"But where's the lawnmower?" she asked, "and the tools?"

"Oh, I found the odd little space in the garage," George said. "And some of the tools needed throwing out."

"Just proves that we did only need one shed," Ruth murmured, as George took Edward to peek at the nest again.

"I built this shed from scratch"

It was surprisingly light and airy in the summerhouse and really quite warm

A s the days went by, Ruth found herself spending more and more time in the summerhouse. Gradually she imported a few bits from the house. First an old kettle and some mugs. Then a small table to put her tea tray on. It really was a very peaceful place to spend an afternoon. Cushions and a footstool followed, and another chair.

"I see you've made it very comfortable," George said one morning as he and Edward walked past on their way to look at the nest.

"They've hatched!" Edward called excitedly, two minutes later. "There are four tiny birds, all skinny and bare-looking, with their eyes tight shut!"

Ruth hurried to the other shed to look.

"It won't be long now," George said,

"and we'll be able to get rid of this shed." He winked at Edward, unseen by his wife. "As you said, no man needs two sheds…"

"Yes, I remember saying that," Ruth said thoughtfully, "a man really does only need one shed." She turned round and started walking back towards the summerhouse, to her tea and her book and her comfortable chair. "And every woman needs one too…"

A WORD FROM THE AUTHOR

"A blackbird nested in our 'extra' shed last spring – giving the shed, and my husband, a few weeks' reprieve – but I'm glad to say we're now a one-shed-family."

Teatime Treat

Glitzy Chocolate Mint Crisps

Preparation time: 20min plus cooling and chilling
Cooking time: 5min
Makes 18

SPARKLY TREAT

Ingredients
- 225g milk or plain chocolate, broken into pieces
- 75g clear mint sweets
- Edible silver balls and small sugar hearts to decorate

● Line a large board with baking parchment. Melt **chocolate** in a heatproof bowl over a saucepan of barely simmering water, then remove from the saucepan and cool for 10min.

● Meanwhile, unwrap the **clear mint sweets** and place inside 2 clean plastic food bags. Holding the end loosely closed, gently crush the sweets using a rolling pin.

● Stir the crushed sweets into the melted chocolate and drop teaspoonfuls of the mixture on to the prepared board. Tap the board on the work surface to form thin round discs. You should be able to make about 18 discs. Decorate with **silver balls** and **sugar hearts** before the chocolate sets.

● Allow to cool, then chill for 30min to set before peeling off the paper to serve.

FUN FOR CHILDREN TO MAKE

RECIPE: KATHRYN HAWKINS PHOTOGRAPHY: LIGHTHOUSE

Heart Of Gold Eyes Of Blue

Be whisked back a century or more to a country fair where a young man and woman find more than they bargained for

By Pamela Kavanagh

Adam Brookfield moved through the fair with his goods and his gear, looking for a suitable pitch. Held each year on the second Wednesday in June, Appleby Fair was proudly proclaimed to have been granted by Royal Charter, but it was Adam's belief that the event had more prosaic origins. Not that he would have argued the point. A man of few words, he had long learned to keep his counsel and it was in his interest to do so now. Adam was a brass-and-copper-smith by trade, and he had ambitions. Appleby, he hoped, would help him realise them.

All around was the clamour of hooves, the rattle of harness and the shouts and laughter of the crowd. Everyone liked a holiday and folks came from near and far to enjoy the fun of the fair, some to pick up a decent animal or two, others content with a fairing as a memento of the day out. Tradesmen, copers and tatters mingled amongst the throng and down by the river the Romany youths were washing their animals in the shallows to smarten them up for selling, whilst gypsy wives toured the aisles with baskets of lucky heather on their arms in the hope of some profitable hawking. The sun beat down, bringing out the mingled smells of warm horseflesh, bruised grass and the waft of strong ale from a nearby vendor.

Adam found a space and set about displaying his wares. He had worked ceaselessly, using his choice moulds to produce the very best adornments for bridle and harness. The moon and stars that were a favourite, the rayed sun, fish, fowl, strange mythical beasts… the turned-down crescent said to ward off the evil eye that no carter or ploughman would be without; all were here to tempt.

The sun brought out the mingled smells of warm horseflesh and bruised grass

From his pitch Adam had a clear view of Top Hill, the straight Roman road where horses and ponies were run out to show their paces. Nearby a blacksmith was hard at work and a saddler was making a deal with a swarthy-faced fellow with an eye for the main chance. **Continued overleaf…**

He searched
for her at
every fair

"Excuse me," said a voice. "Do you have any candle-snuffers?"

Adam straightened from placing a plaque with his name on it amongst the glittering wares. A girl stood before him. Dainty and pert, she had hair the colour of autumn beech-woods and the bluest eyes he had ever seen.

"It's for Gran'ma, you see," the speaker went on eagerly. "She had a pot one Granfer had given her and when we were small she'd let us play with it and it got chipped and cracked over time, then the other week Gran'ma was looking after our Betsy's youngest and she gave it her to keep her quiet and the little madam went and dropped it and it broke, and our Eddie said a brass one would stand up better to wear and tear."

She paused for breath and Adam, hard-pressed to follow the diatribe, ran a hand in confusion over his unruly crop of curls. "A candle-snuffer? Aye, I do have them, though not with me. It's all harness decoration here."

"Oh, I see." The girl's face fell.

"Mine are just plain things, nothing but hollowed out lumps of brass, really."

"Oh. Gran'ma's was a lady in a beautiful crinoline gown. Still, a plain one would be better than nothing." The girl had a light, fluting voice that Adam found captivating. "'Twill be the anniversary of Gran'ma's birth at the end of the month. She'll be eighty summers old… or thereabouts, she isn't quite sure. We thought to give it her then."

"Happen you'll find what you're looking for elsewhere," Adam said kindly, aware of the potential customers that

"Odd creatures, women," the shepherd said

were gathering to study his stall.

"I don't think so. You're the only brass-and-copper-smith here. I've come all the way from Kirkby Thore especially."

"That's a good step. I came through your village on my way from Penrith."

"Penrith?" Hope shone in her eyes.

"Do you have a shop there?"

"Well, no." Adam caught his breath. This was his goal, what he had worked and saved for. In his mind's eye he saw the premises he coveted; a modest but adequate establishment on the main street, with his name over the door and smithy at the back, living quarters above the shop. It was coming up for rent in the not so distant future, hence the need to get together the down-payment.

"Are't doing business today, Smith?" enquired a gruff voice at his elbow. A man was eyeing up a set of terret bells and Adam collected himself.

"Aye, sir. I've more of those, similar, if you're interested…"

The girl turned sadly away. The last Adam glimpsed of her was a bright flame of auburn hair disappearing amongst the milling crowds.

Trade was brisk and by midday the money-bag at his waist felt gratifyingly heavy. Breakfast by now was a distant memory and Adam's stomach growled, so – leaving the man on the next booth to keep an eye on his stall – Adam went to the tavern for a noontide pie and tankard of ale. As he ate he thought about the candle-snuffer girl, her dimpled cheeks and forget-me-not eyes.

"Shall you be staying on for tonight's revels, Smith?" enquired a fellow at the bar, who by his checked waistcoat and the crimson dicklo at his throat looked to be a tatter. "There's dancing."

"I hadn't thought." Adam wondered what it would be like to dance with the

after a long day, smiling face across the hearth of an evening, sons to take over my farm when I'm gone – what more could a fellow want?"

"A deaf ear for when the missus has got a shrewish mood on her!" someone said, and everyone laughed.

Adam left the smoky thrall of the taproom and headed back across the fair ground, throwing a glance round for the girl, but she was nowhere to be seen. By now he was regretting not having dealt better with the request that was made out of the kindness of her heart.

Kirkby Thore would have a market. He could have arranged to meet her with the item; made a deal, offering two for the price of one if she would spread the word where the candle-snuffers had come

As he ate his noontide pie, he thought of the girl and her forget-me-not eyes

girl. She was so dainty she'd be like thistledown in his arms. "Maybe."

"Likely you'll find yourself a sweetheart, Smith," put in a blunt-faced farmer in gaiters and cloth cap. "Many a fellow has got himself a wife at Appleby."

Adam shrugged. "Don't know about that. A wife holds a man back."

"That's true," put in old Seth the shepherd from where he sat with his dogs at his feet. A bachelor right down to the holes in his socks, he drew deeply on a clay pipe. "Strange creatures, women. You never know where you are with them."

"Twaddle!" the farmer returned emphatically. "I'm a married man myself. A hot meal on the table when I get in

from. All was good for business. He had not even enquired her name, and it struck him that he would like to know who she was. He'd like it very much indeed.

Throughout the afternoon, to the background crack of the auctioneer's gavel and shouts of "oi, oi, oi!" from the auction ground, Adam continued to make sales. By the time sun sank behind a distant line of woodland every item had gone and Adam had even taken some orders. All the while he had kept an eye out for a fiery mop of hair, but in this respect he was not lucky. The girl did not appear again.

Novelty candle-snuffers, he mused as he hoisted his gear onto his shoulder in **Continued overleaf…**

Continued from previous page

preparation for the twelve-mile tramp home. On his way out he passed a stall selling shawl pins and brooches fashioned like flowers. One, a cluster of forget-me-nots, was exactly the colour of the girl's eyes and on impulse he bought it, dropping it into his pocket. She had given him an idea for a brand new line, and for that he was grateful.

"Did you get one?" her brother asked

Lisbeth trudged homeward, her unspent pennies jangling in her purse. She had gone back to the brassware stall but the smith had not been there. The rest of the afternoon had slipped away and all she had bought was a fairing for Mam, a shawl pin to replace the ugly thing Mam secured her shawl with at present. Really it was the sort of thing a lad bought for his sweetheart but it was the prettiest there. Lisbeth wished a lad would give her a love-token but it wasn't likely, as Mam said she talked too much and if there was anything a man hated in a wife it was a prattler. Lisbeth had tried often to curb her tongue but it was hopeless, so she had more or less resigned herself to being a spinster like Minnie Robs across the way.

Reaching home, she saw her brother Eddie sorting out withy wands for the basket-making business that he and their father ran from the cottage.

"Did you get one?" Eddie asked.

"No. There was only one stall selling brass-and-copperware and the smith just had horse-gear on display – though he does have candle-snuffers back home."

"Did you find out where he's from?"

"Yes, Penrith. His name's Adam Brookfield and he's a master brass-and-copper-smith, it said so on the stall."

"He'll have a shop, then."

"I was asking him about that and he said no and there was a queue building up so I came away."

"Happen he'll have a stall on Penrith Market," Eddie said. "Why don't you see? Go on Friday."

"Can't. I promised our Betsy I'd see after her little'ns while she does some dairy-work at the farm. It'll have to be another time."

"We've got till the month end. Did you like the fair?"

"Oh, yes! There were stalls and entertainments. I wanted to stay for the dancing but it was getting late. Maybe just as well. Who'd want to dance with a chatterbox like me?"

"Someone might, providing he could get a word in edgeways to ask you!" Eddie said with a grin.

Counting his earnings from Appleby Fair, Adam realised that he had nearly reached his target. Another pound or two and he would have enough for the down-payment on the Appleby premises, and leave some over for a few necessary sticks of furniture.

Next morning he was up with the sun, leaving his lodgings for the smithy opposite, stoking up the furnace. From a battered wooden box he removed his smaller moulds that would normally produce the popular novelty bells, but with a little adapting could become candle-snuffers – far more appealing than the usual nugget of brass fashioned from melt left over from the day. He set to work and by sunset, a choice selection of candle-snuffers stood on his shelf.

On the windowsill he had placed the brooch, and the glass of the flowers had sparkled like blue fire in the sunlight, catching his eye as he worked, reminding him of the one who had been his inspiration. Tomorrow being market day, he packed up his goods for the stall,

"Oh, yes. A woman on a drapery booth said Adam had given up his stall and got a shop. I went all over Penrith but there was no brass and copper shop there. I found out where his lodgings were and went there, but the landlady said he'd packed up and gone at the weekend. He's given up the lease on the smithy and all so it looks –"

"Did the landlady say where he'd gone to?" Eddie interrupted.

"She didn't know. She said he was the best lodger she'd ever had; always paid up on the dot." Lisbeth sighed. "Isn't that typical? He was nice, too."

"Who's nice?" said a voice from the doorway. Mam stood there, shopping baskets in her hands, the Appleby pin glinting on her shawl.

"Just somebody at the fair. The pin looks lovely, Mam. Lads were buying them for their girls." Lisbeth sighed again. "I should be so lucky!"

"There, child. You've got a kind heart. One of these days it might happen."

Lisbeth thought of the tall figure

There was a steadiness about Adam that made other lads she knew seem wanting

adding his new line to the usual selection of brass and copper ornaments, bed-warmers, candlesticks, companion sets and toasting forks. After some thought, he removed one of the candle-snuffers and stowed it away in his pocket.

"Well?" Eddie looked up from the basket he was weaving as his sister entered the workshop.

"He wasn't there. I looked all over the marketplace – everywhere."

"Did you ask where he might be?"

behind the stall and swallowed hard. Adam Brookfield had seemed different to the lads she knew. There had been a steadiness about him that made the others seem wanting. He had looked at her in a way that made her feel she was the prettiest maid in the fair.

"Looks like we'll have to forget Gran'ma's candle-snuffer," Eddie said once their mother had gone.

"Yes, I fear that it does," Lisbeth replied dolefully.

Continued overleaf…

Continued from previous page

andle-snuffer, ma'am? I've only this Dutch girl left." Adam smiled at the housewife across the counter of the shop.

"I'll take it. And shall you be having any more?"

"Surely. Once I'm settled in I'll try out some new ideas."

"I'll look forward to it. Oh, and while I'm here I'll take a companion set. One of those with horses' heads will look nice on the hearth."

The customer paid for her purchases and left, shop-bell jangling after her. Adam rearranged the items on the shelf, spreading them out to fill the gaps. Trade had been good and he would have to see about replenishing the depleted stock. First, he had that other matter to attend to. Last Thursday he had shut up shop early and gone to Kirkby Thore in the hope of spotting the girl in the market place. The visit had been in vain and Adam had to think again.

On Sunday morning, after dousing himself under the pump in the backyard, Adam pulled on a clean shirt and his suit of woollen worsted and set off for the

Would you mind very much walking a little way with me?"

People were looking and hastily Lisbeth took the proffered arm. "What was it you wanted, Adam? I may call you Adam, mayn't I?"

"Aye. I don't know your name."

She blushed. "It's Lisbeth."

"'Tis a pretty name." Pausing on the path, Adam drew from his pocket the special candle-snuffer. "Lisbeth – I've made you this."

"Oh!" She took it wonderingly, turning it about in her hands. Sunlight struck off gleaming brass, illuminating the craftsmanship in every detail of the face and fold of the skirts. "A crinoline lady! Oh, Adam, she's so beautiful. Gran'ma will be so thrilled."

"I searched for you. I came here to the Thursday market but you weren't there."

"I've been seeing after our Betsy's little'ns on and off. I came looking for you too. I really wanted the candle-snuffer for Gran'ma and Eddie thought to try at Penrith, but they said you'd gone."

"Only as far as Appleby. I've just

"A crinoline lady! Oh Adam, she's so beautiful. Gran'ma will be thrilled"

village in the fold of the fells. Waiting at the church gates, he saw the bright head of hair immediately amongst the departing congregation.

She was alone, Adam saw thankfully.

"'Morning," he greeted as she passed under the lyche-arch.

She stopped short. "Oh – it's you!"

"I wanted to see you.

opened up a shop there." He smiled.

"At Appleby? I was looking in the wrong place, then! Adam, you must let me pay you for this."

"You don't owe me a thing." Hesitantly, Adam told her about his success with the new line. "'Tis early days yet but I reckon it's a winner and it's all thanks to you. Making novelty candle-snuffers would never have entered my head – so let's call it a deal."

"A deal it is! What a shame you had a

"Your talk puts me in mind of the swallows"

it seemed that time hung suspended.

Clearing his throat, he said, "I like your talk. It puts me in mind of the swallows that chitter-chatter outside my window. Lisbeth, there's a fair next week at Dufton. Will you come with me? There'll be dancing."

"I'd love that," she said, beaming.

Things went from strength to strength. By the time Appleby Fair came round again Adam's business had grown and he had his girl on his arm. When night fell and the fiddler struck up with his twinkling bow, drawing the dancers onto the floor, Adam pulled from his pocket the forget-me-not brooch he had treasured so long.

"Lisbeth, I'd like you to have this. 'Tis nothing much, but it means a lot to me."

"Oh! I never expected to get one of these, ever. Adam, thank you!"

"Let me pin it on for you… There." Adam smiled in satisfaction and added quietly, "Will you marry me?"

Speechless for once, all Lisbeth could do was nod happily.

After that, whenever June came round and the shouted *oi, oi, oi* and clatter of hooves marked yet another gathering along the old Roman road, Adam would remember that first time. The fluting voice, the forget-me-not eyes, and the day he found happiness at Appleby Fair.

wasted journey that day. Didn't you think to ask on the market? You'd only have needed to mention my hair and anyone would have directed you to Bournes the basket-makers."

"Your folks are in a trade, too? Well I never! But I'd not have gone chasing you up like that."

"I wouldn't have minded. I'm used to being called Carrots. Well – that or Chatterbox."

Adam threw a glance at her flowing mass of hair. "There's nothing carroty about that. It's like burnished copper. Truth is, Lisbeth, I'm a retiring sort of fellow. Never have much to say as a rule."

"And I'm just the opposite."

There was a silence while they looked thoughtfully at each other. High overhead, a lark was warbling and the sun brought out the scents of wayside flowers and grass. To Adam, gazing into the earnest, dimpled face upturned to his,

A WORD FROM THE AUTHOR

"I was given an old brass candle-snuffer. Polishing it up, I wondered what its story could be – and the idea for *Heart Of Gold, Eyes Of Blue* was born."

Taking Care Of Maisie

Are any of the elderly lady's concerned relatives what they seem? Enjoy a delicious shiver as you read on to find out!

By Annie Preston

Lucy stood at the curve of the stairs as her niece Alice and her husband, Stan, entered through the front door. The bright moonbeams forced their way through the stained glass, throwing a pale spectrum of colour along the hallway. Stan ran his hands along the wall, as if trying to catch the rainbow as it ran flat against the paper.

As the pair walked down the hall, they still hadn't spotted the elderly relative watching silently.

Alice was the daughter of Lucy's brother-in-law, and when she had arrived in his twilight years, to a much younger wife, he was thrilled. He spoiled the child from the day she was born. She grew into a confident but overbearing woman, not suffering fools gladly, or in any other way. She walked with an air of self-possession, constantly tossing her blonde hair over her shoulder, whilst her aquiline nose was made perfectly for looking down – which she did often, and at everyone.

Stan, on the other hand, was a perfect foil for his wife. A haphazard person, he constantly needed direction. If it wasn't for his wife putting ideas into his head, his time on earth would have been spent continuously climbing out of a chaotic jumble.

Everyone wondered what Alice had seen in this befuddled man; the most generous thing to be said about him was that he was a fool.

Closing the door behind him, Stan reassured his wife, telling her what she wanted to hear. He rifled through the hall cupboard as he spoke, searching for anything of interest or value.

"Look, Alice, everyone will realise that

"You are her only relative that could cope. The rest of the family are ancient"

you want to look after Maisie. It stands to reason. You are her only relative that could cope. All the rest of the family are ancient, ready to pop their own clogs at any minute. You are next in line. Now stop worrying. It will be fine. You'll see."

They were still unaware of the grey-frocked Lucy as they passed into her only surviving child's room. The downstairs lounge had been converted to house the

Alice's nose was perfect for looking down

bed and other essentials when Maisie's stroke had made it impossible for her to climb the steep double flight of stairs to her own bedroom.

Lucy made her way downstairs and peeked around the door to see Alice bending over the bed-ridden woman. Maisie tried to avoid Alice as she put her lips close to her ear.

"Don't worry, Auntie, Stan and I will look after you. Everything will be fine now we're here." She stroked the clammy forehead, smoothing the grey curls back towards the pillow.

Maisie tried to speak, but the stroke had rendered one side of her face useless and her words were strained and meaningless.

"Now don't upset yourself, Auntie," comforted Stan, bending his angular **Continued overleaf…**

Continued from previous page

frame over the immobile woman, blocking the moonlight as the rays streamed in through the bay window. "Alice will make you a nice cup of tea, whilst I tidy the house up a little bit. We'll put the heating on for a while; it seems very chilly in here this evening," he added as he turned away, holding on to his wife's elbow as he steered her towards the kitchen at the back of the house.

"It's so cold in here…"

Lucy had positioned herself behind the kitchen door, where she would be hidden from the two younger relatives' view. They were still completely unaware of her presence. She breathed quietly, not daring to move in case of discovery.

She worried about her daughter. Lucy couldn't look after her, and she now needed constant help. The home-carer had been coming in three times a day for the past week since Maisie had returned from hospital, and a neighbour had stayed overnight once or twice, but that was only useful in the interim – and the poor soul needed even more care since falling out of bed two days previously.

"But," Lucy reminded herself, "our problem is solved now. From today

never think it was the warmest autumn we've had for fifteen years."

Alice put boiling water into the china cup that contained a solitary tea bag. She turned to Stanley, now sifting his way through kitchen cabinets.

"For goodness' sake leave things alone for now and pass the sugar. She takes three. Hopefully the sweetness will mask the taste of her 'medication.'"

Alice smiled as she sprinkled powder, alongside the sugar, into the Sunday-best crockery.

Quietly Lucy came from her hiding place and stood between the couple. She looked up at Stanley's thin face and stroked the unshaven cheek. She then

"Leave things alone and pass the sugar. Hopefully it will mask the taste…"

Maisie will be looked after properly; she'll be warm, fed, and well cared for, until she recovers enough to look after herself."

Alice looked around the well-kept kitchen and shivered. "It does seem terribly cold in here, Stan – you would

turned to her niece and ran her fingers through her long blonde hair, blowing on the pretty but stunned face as she did so.

"What on earth was that?" shrieked Alice, flattening her hair back down onto her head. "Did you feel it, Stan? I swear something touched me."

"Don't be silly, woman. It was the breeze from the window. That's all. Come on, let's get this over with," barked Stan, picking up the faded floral tray that carried both Maisie's steaming tea and her possible fate.

Lucy followed the pair into the make-shift bedroom, keeping pace and settling herself next to her daughter's bed. She looked down at her, wishing she could do more for her now elderly first-born child. But perhaps she could…

The tray was placed on the small table everyone to think we're mad?" she hissed at her husband. "The old bird probably didn't have much to leave us anyway."

Lucy stood by the doorway watching the ingrate relatives disappearing down the driveway. She turned her attention to the two people behind her as they gently placed a now smiling Maisie onto a stretcher.

The ambulance driver spoke gently to her. "We'll soon have you tucked up in bed, my lovely, as snug as a bug in a rug.

The ambulance driver spoke gently as the woman fussed with Maisie's case

that sat immediately in front of Lucy. As Alice bent forward to take the tea, Lucy beat her to it and gently lifted the cup towards her niece's lips.

Alice shrieked for the second time in five minutes. The sound that issued from her husband's mouth was a slightly higher pitch. Startled, Lucy dropped the cup, the contents spilling over the legs of both pretenders.

The care and concern the couple had felt for dear Auntie Maisie just half an hour before had evaporated as they fought to reach the front door, each before the other. As they scuttled over the threshold into the warm evening air, they met an ambulance driver and a carer coming towards the house.

Stan, after staggering along the gravel footpath, stood to his full, skinny height and announced to no one in particular, "That house is haunted! It's bewitched, and it just attacked us."

Alice tidied her clothes as she tried to regain some dignity.

"Shut up, you idiot. So you want

And Effie here will take good care of you." He nodded his head towards the middle-aged lady who was fussing with Maisie's small suitcase, and holding her patient's limp hand.

"We'll look after you in Sunnybank for as long as you need us to. And you'll be home again, under your own steam, before you know it – and what a beautiful, cosy house it is too."

Lucy stood to one side, allowing the man to push her daughter out into the moonlight. Gently she kissed her face with a touch as gentle as a whisper.

Maisie smiled at the fading image of her mother, knowing that everything would be safe until she returned home.

A WORD FROM THE AUTHOR

"One of my hobbies is wandering round cemeteries, and one of my favourite writers is crime thriller author Ian Rankin! A truly inspiring combination!"

Don't Look Back

Before starting her new journey, Flora knew she'd have to confront the past

By Susan Sarapuk

lora stood outside the gate and looked at the pink house. A tangle of bushes formed a hedge, beyond which was a carefully manicured lawn and a mulberry tree. The tree was taller than she remembered – although it must have been pruned over the years, for she'd been nine when she'd left this place.

Flora had known she'd have to come home – not to the flat in London she returned to every day, but here, to her childhood home.

Helena, her best friend, had encouraged her to do it. "It might help you sort out things."

Flora turned to look down the lane where sand banked against the edges. At the end the Tarmac petered out onto the beach. She could just about see the ocean creeping onto the shore. She recalled that from the bedroom window, you could see over the tops of the trees to the long expanse of beach.

Funny how things changed and left you wondering when it had happened, and how you had come to this point.

Guy had left her, gone back to the US.

"You know I'd stay if I could, Flora, but it's work," he'd said.

But Flora knew it wasn't just work; it was where he was from, the pull of home.

She'd visited there: the washed-out pastel colours of the shoreline, the clapboard houses, dog roses and American flags in the gardens and a lighthouse on the headland.

She'd met Guy through work – he'd been on a six-month secondment. It was his eyes she'd first noticed, laughing eyes. He was full of enthusiasm for life, always looking to explore and experience new things.

"I don't know London," he'd said one day. "Fancy showing me around?"

It was as easy as that; they quickly became friends and then a bit more than friends. It was the easiest relationship she'd ever had.

He told her about his family.

"I've got a sister, Mitzi; she's in college. And Sam, my brother, he's eight. Bit of an afterthought on my parents' part. But he's great. He's gonna be a football player, I swear. What about your family?"

That's when she'd had to admit that she was alone.

"I'm an only child. Both my parents are

Guy had only known a happy family life, but her expectations were different

Flora turned away and headed to the beach

dead now, but they divorced when I was young."

He'd looked at her sadly, as if being in such a position was beyond his comprehension.

And now she stood looking up at the house she'd left that day, with one case full of her favourite toys and her mother clutching her other hand as they waited for Dave, the local taxi driver, to arrive and take them off to the city.

Guy had only ever known a happy family life, and he expected one in his future. But Flora realised that her expectations were different.

"There's something sad about you," he'd said one day when they were sitting on Tower Green munching sandwiches. "It's almost as if something's missing." **Continued overleaf…**

Continued from previous page

He never tired of seeing the Tower of London. "Can you believe this place? You Brits don't realise what you've got."

Flora had to admit he had a point – although she lived and worked in London she'd never done any of the touristy things.

And then, after Guy had gone, Helena had said that she ought to go back and revisit the past.

The past was another country. And yet, as Flora peered over the hedge it was as if she'd only left yesterday.

Was she going to open the gate, walk up the path and knock on the door? She was afraid that the reality wouldn't live up to the memories she'd built up over the years.

So Flora turned away from the gate and walked down the lane to the beach.

On the way she passed the shop where she used to buy iced lollies, with its colourful display of buckets and spades and inflatables suspended from the troughing, and the shed with its canoes and deckchairs for hire. Nothing much had changed here.

It was early in the season, the sun not yet hot enough to warm the sea, yet there were a few families spread out along the shore. Flora strolled along the beach enjoying the wide sky, the shoosh of the waves and the smell of ozone, pretending that she wasn't running away.

Once upon a time, this had been her world where anything seemed possible and she'd been happy. In those days before her parents had argued to the point where they could no longer live together, and she'd felt uprooted, cast into the maelstrom of the city.

All those years she'd tried not to think of leaving everything she'd loved behind, as if remembering would break her heart. But Guy had been right – there was

Would it be how she remembered?

something missing and it was time to come to terms with her past.

At the far end of the beach stood a rocky headland. She remembered climbing the rocks when she was a child. There was a place where the rocks had been hollowed out to form a bridge across the entrance to a cave which her friends had challenged each other to cross. The drop to the sand below wouldn't seem that far now, yet as children it had appeared frightening.

Flora began to climb the path that led up the side of the cliff. Higher up she could see a group of children climbing.

The sound of crying suddenly alerted her to the presence of someone. There was a young girl perched on a rock just below her, close to where the bridge spanned the cave. For a moment Flora paused before leaving the path and climbing down.

"Hello." She drew up alongside the girl. "Are you okay?"

"They've left me," she choked, her cheeks wet with tears. "They said I was chicken. No one would come back down with me. They wouldn't wait for me."

Flora looked around, quickly assessing the situation.

"Are you scared to cross the bridge?" Wide-eyed with fear, the girl nodded.

"I used to do it when I was your age," Flora said. The first time she'd been scared, she remembered, but Richard Morris's taunting had made her rustle up some courage from somewhere and she'd run across, thinking the sooner she got to the other side the less likely it was that she would fall. "I was terrified too," she confessed. "But once you've done it…"

Flora wondered whether she should be encouraging such recklessness with the current obsession over health and safety, but children needed to flirt with danger

"Don't look down!" Flora advised.

The girl choked another cry as she teetered on the brink. "I want to do it!" she cried.

From up above came a shout. "Hey Keira, are you coming or what?"

The girl threw Flora a desperate look. Then Flora saw her grit her teeth, summon up her courage, and step out with arms extended for balance.

"That's it, you can do it."

Laughing with relief, the girl made it to Flora's side.

"I did it!" she squealed.

"Hey, Keira did it!" came another cry from above.

Keira began to climb, eager to join her friends now. She didn't even look back to say thank you. That was the joy of youth, Flora supposed, always focused on the next thing.

Once upon a time this had been her world, where anything seemed possible

to feel a sense of achievement, to grow, to reach out for possibilities.

"Come on!" She jumped up from the rock. "Let's do it!"

"But you're old!" the girl protested.

"Well, if an oldie can do it…" and Flora stepped out and walked across the bridge.

"What if I fall?" The girl quivered.

"Don't think of that. Just think of doing it, of catching up with your friends, of being one of the gang. Say, 'I can do this too'. You're as good as them, aren't you?"

"Of course I am!" the girl said huffily. She stood up, moved tentatively towards the bridge and peered over.

Flora looked out to sea. *You could run away from challenges or overcome them*, she thought, her mind made up.

She retraced her steps to the pink house, pausing outside before determinedly opening the gate and striding up to the front door.

A young woman with a baby on her hip answered her knock.

"Hello, my name's Flora Marshall." She introduced herself. "I used to live here when I was a child and wondered if I might look around."

"There was a Gerald Marshall here, wasn't there?" The woman looked delighted to see her. "He owned the **Continued overleaf…**

Continued from previous page

house before the person we bought it from. I've been doing some research while I'm stuck at home with the baby. Come in. I'm Laura."

Flora stepped into the hallway. She could smell lunch cooking and lavender furniture polish.

"Have a look around," said the young woman. "I'll put some coffee on."

Of course it was different; Flora had known it would be, but some things were the same, like the chip in the door jamb to the living room she'd made when she'd ridden her tricycle into it as a three-year-old. The shelves in the pantry under the stairs remained the same; the stone slab even covered with the same printed oilcloth. And upstairs, in what had been her bedroom and was now a nursery, the view from the window hadn't changed at all, with the sand dunes and the blue sky and the ships on the horizon.

Flora stood in the centre of the room and looked around. It was a happy house and, contrary to what she'd dreaded, she didn't feel sad. Whatever had happened was in the past. It was her life and she'd survived it. The past was another country and she'd moved on.

Laura was pouring out coffee as Flora wandered into the kitchen, every part of which was new, from the units to the colour on the walls, from the tiled splashbacks to the blinds at the window overlooking a vegetable garden.

"I expect it's changed a lot." Laura smiled. "Were you happy here?"

"Yes, I was," Flora admitted.

Perhaps if her parents had stayed it would have all soured for her. They weren't happy together. But it didn't mean that she wouldn't be happy, that it

Memories flooded back

The view from her bedroom hadn't changed at all

wouldn't all work out for her.

"Where do you live?" Laura asked.

"I'm in London at the moment, but next month I'm moving to the US. I'm getting married."

She was looking forward to exchanging London for the washed-out Massachusetts shoreline, clapboard houses, dog roses, US flags and the lighthouse on the headland.

She was going to Guy and Mitzi and Sam and Jack and Deborah, her new family. And now she knew that she was going to be happy. She was going to another country.

A WORD FROM THE AUTHOR

"This story was inspired by a beach I know on the Gower coast and an interest in how our past can influence our present."

ILLUSTRATIONS: JIM DEWAR

Teatime Treat

EAT AS A PUD, TOO!

Raspberry Frangipane Slices

REAL FRUIT PIECES

Ingredients

- 500g ready-made, all-butter, shortcrust pastry
- 115g butter, softened
- 115g caster sugar
- 2 eggs
- 2tbsp double cream
- 115g ground almonds
- 2tbsp flour
- 150g fresh raspberries
- Icing sugar

Preparation time: 25min
Cooking time: 35min

● Preheat the oven to 200°C, Fan Oven 180°C, Gas Mark 6. Place a baking sheet in the oven to heat. Roll out the **pastry** and line a 17x28cm oblong flan tin with it. Prick the base and chill until the filling is ready.

● Cream the **butter** and add the **sugar**. Beat until light and soft. Beat the **egg** and stir into the mixture a little at a time. Add the **double cream**. Stir in the **almonds** and **flour**.

● Spread the filling into the pastry case and lay the **raspberries** on top, pressing them down gently.

● Bake in the oven on the hot baking sheet for 15min until the top is beginning to brown. Turn the oven down to 180°C, Fan Oven 160°C, Gas Mark 4 and cook for a further 15-20min or until the frangipane is cooked. Remove from the oven and allow to cool in the tin. Just before serving, dust with **icing sugar**. Serve warm or cold.

RECIPE: FIONA BURRELL PHOTOGRAPHY: LIGHTHOUSE

Three Wishes

A life-changing experience at the car boot sale? No – our down-to-earth heroine couldn't really believe it, either…

By Kat Parkhurst

Hey, I'm Kylie – cool to meet you, and all that. Now, what are your three wishes?"

"I'm – er – sorry…" Pam stared at the teenager who'd seemingly appeared from nowhere. She must have been serving behind one of the other stalls. She hadn't noticed her before, which was odd because she was hard to miss. She was wearing a grubby red and gold headdress strung with small coins, a red bra top and floaty, fringed harem pants. The ensemble, and her bare feet, were streaked with black marks.

Pam was only just quick enough to avoid the red-tipped fingernails.

"Hold it right there, young lady. I already know I'm not dreaming. I'm far too hot." She waved the hand that wasn't holding the lamp in front of her face. "Are you a friend of my grandson's? His name's Jack."

"Not that I know of – is he fit?" Kylie smiled. She was pretty when she smiled and Pam found herself softening. It might be an odd conversation, but it was certainly livening up the rather dull car boot sale. She hadn't found a single bargain since she'd arrived and had been contemplating heading home.

"This is a wind-up, right?" asked Pam, who had three teenage grandchildren

"Do I know you?" Pam demanded, rather suspiciously.

"I'm a genie." Kylie gave an impatient gesture towards the small copper lamp Pam was holding. "And there's no need to look down your nose. You'd be grubby if you'd spent the last two months in that."

"Hmm, very droll." Pam took a deep breath. She prided herself on being able to communicate with the younger generation, having three teenage grandchildren. "This is a wind-up, right?"

Kylie frowned and pinched herself with a hand much cleaner than the rest of her outfit would have suggested. "Well, I'm certainly not dreaming. How about you?"

A scattering of people were milling about, bargaining with stall holders and rummaging through the bric-a-brac. Pam decided it wouldn't hurt to play along with Kylie for a while.

"So you're going to grant me three wishes, are you?" She made to put the lamp back on the trestle table.

"Only if you're the new owner of that lamp – otherwise the wishes wouldn't rightfully be yours."

"I see," Pam murmured. Well, it was certainly the best sales pitch she'd heard today. Where was the harm?

She handed over fifty pence to the **Continued overleaf…**

"Only if you're the new owner of that lamp…"

young woman behind the stall, who winked as she thanked her – no doubt Kylie's partner in crime – and then turned back to Kylie. She'd half expected her to be gone now she'd got her to buy the lamp, but she was still there, tapping her foot on the scrubby grass, her eyebrows raised in patronising arches.

"Any chance of telling me your first wish? I haven't got all day."

"Well, I don't want to waste it. That's what usually happens, isn't it? People are so surprised to meet a genie that they usually throw away their first wish on something trivial they didn't even want that much – like, say, wishing they had a bit more time to think."

"Is that a wish?"

"Certainly not. I'm thinking about it." Pam winked to show she didn't actually believe anything would happen anyway and she was merely playing along. "I suppose wishing for a lifetime supply of wishes is out of the question?"

Kylie nodded emphatically. "Against the rules, I'm afraid."

"All right then. Well – I wish I was rich beyond my wildest dreams."

"You'll get a surprise in the post next week," Kylie said with a grin and suddenly she was off, skipping away through the small crowd.

"Hang on a minute – what about my other wishes?" Pam called after her, but there was no reply.

She laughed quietly to herself. Well, that had been fun, anyway. She glanced down at the little lamp in her hand. It was pretty enough, and had *Made in Brighton* stamped on the bottom. She'd keep it as a memento.

Pam had no post all week, which was no great surprise, but she was just rushing out on Friday morning to take Jack to college because it was the day Eileen started work early, when the postman stopped her at the gate.

"Here's one for you, Mrs B." He handed her a white envelope.

She thanked him and stuffed it in her bag, not even thinking about it again until she got home and opened it… and discovered she'd had a win on the premium bonds. A big win.

Her legs felt shaky as she looked at the letter. Oh, my – there was enough here to help Eileen out so that she didn't have to work so hard; enough to put her grandchildren through Uni without them having student loans – and there'd still be plenty left over for a holiday.

She looked at the little lamp, which she'd left on the kitchen windowsill for want of a better place to put it, and wondered if it could possibly be a coincidence. It had to be. But just in case it wasn't, she moved the lamp to her glass cupboard. It looked odd in amongst her Wedgwood but at least it'd be safe.

Having confirmed with the premium bond people that the letter was indeed genuine – she'd had her doubts – she took her whole family out for a slap-up meal to celebrate.

"You could buy a country cottage like you've always wanted, Gran!" Emma suggested, her blue eyes sparkling.

"Or how about a world cruise – hey, actually, we could *all* go on a world cruise, couldn't we?"

"*You* couldn't, Jack – you've got your accountancy exams to take." That was

She paid the woman behind the stall

"Or how about a world cruise – hey, we could *all* go on a world cruise now!"

Rosie, her eldest grandchild – always the sensible one.

"Never mind about my accountancy exams – that's a boring job anyway. Gran wouldn't want me to waste my life doing something I hated, would you, Gran?" Jack blew her a lazy kiss. He'd always been able to wind her round his little finger. "Don't suppose I could have a sub, could I? I'm up to my overdraft limit."

"Don't be so selfish, Jack. You know I need a car." Rosie frowned. "Mum can't put me on her insurance indefinitely."

By the end of the evening Pam had a headache and she was beginning to wish she'd never mentioned her win.

"They'll calm down, don't worry," Eileen reassured her. "But I don't think you should get carried away with the handouts, Mum. Having a lot of money sometimes causes more problems than it solves, you know."

Wasn't that the truth, Pam thought some weeks later, when she'd finally sorted out settlements that no one was particularly happy with and had booked herself an Arctic cruise.

It was while she was on the cruise listening to one of the speakers talk about the icebergs they would see the following day that Pam inadvertently made her second wish.

"Oh, John, I wish you were still here. I'd give anything to see you again – even if it were just for half an hour."

And in the next moment, there she was, sitting in the familiarity of ward twenty-three beside John's bed, trying to ignore the beeps of the machines and the hospital smell and the dryness of her mouth because she was so scared their time together was running out.

She'd spread out some holiday
Continued overleaf…

Continued from previous page

brochures, which she'd picked up on her way in to visit, hoping they'd cheer him up. John was propped up on pillows so he could see them.

"I've always fancied an Arctic cruise," she murmured, and he squeezed her hand gently.

"I'll take you on one when I get out of here. We'll go check out some icebergs."

"What do you think they're like, love?"

"Blooming cold, I expect." He smiled at her, his eyes still as blue as the day she'd first met him, even though his face was gaunt and pale and they both knew there'd be no Arctic cruise. Not for John. He was in the last stages of his illness.

"I love you so much," she whispered.

"I love you, too. We'll go on that Arctic cruise, one day. I'll be with you in spirit even if not in body."

Those were the last words he said before he slipped away from her.

"Time to go now." The nurse was tapping her shoulder and Pam turned with her eyes full of tears.

"Time to go now. Are you okay, love?"

Pam realised she was looking into the eyes not of a Macmillan nurse, but of the man who'd just given the lecture. He was tall and silver-haired and his face was kind and anxious.

"I think you must have dozed off," he said with a smile. "Don't worry, I shan't take it personally."

"I'm so sorry." Pam scrambled to her feet. "It wasn't your talk – truly – I must be more tired than I thought."

How had that happened? How come one minute she'd been in a hospital with John and the next she'd been back on board the cruise ship?

Had she really just used up her second wish – or had she simply fallen asleep and dreamed that she'd been back with John? She hoped it was the latter because if she hadn't dreamed it, she'd wasted the wish because she'd only asked for half an hour.

The memory of her late husband's much-loved face was almost enough to make her squander her last wish on asking for her life all over again, but she wasn't sure that was such a good idea.

Should she wish to live her whole life over again?

I *shall have to be careful to use my last wish wisely,* Pam decided, once she was back at home again. It was a revelation – although perhaps it shouldn't have been – to find that being rich beyond her wildest dreams and even being able to turn back time hadn't made her happy.

she saw Kylie again. This time she was dressed in jeans and a T-shirt but she still had grubby bare feet. She was talking to someone in the queue at the burger van.

With an excited knot in her stomach, Pam hurried across and tapped her on the shoulder.

"Excuse me, I'd like to say thank you,"

"World peace? That might have been a bit too much to ask, even for Kylie…"

"I don't know why you're so surprised, Mum," Eileen said, as they shared cake and lattes in an expensive coffee bar that had just opened in their local shopping centre. "It's a fact of life that you can't buy happiness – you used to tell me that when I was little and pestering you for a new toy you and Dad couldn't afford."

Pam smiled and put her hand over her daughter's. "I don't feel very wise," she confessed. "I'm wondering if I should have asked for world peace or something. That would have been far less selfish, wouldn't it?"

"It might have been too much, even for Kylie." Eileen's eyes were soft. "Have you ever seen her again? I thought genies had to be present for each wish."

"It would appear not," Pam said and they both laughed at the weak attempt at a joke. "I think maybe I should keep it simple this time."

"So what will you wish for?"

"I think my last wish is that we can all be happy – you, me and the kids, that's a sensible wish, isn't it?"

"Very sensible," Eileen said with an affectionate smile.

P am was at a car boot sale the following Saturday when she thought

she began, but then the young woman turned and Pam realised to her embarrassment that it wasn't Kylie, but someone who looked very similar.

"I'm sorry," she murmured. "I thought you were someone else."

The young woman smiled. "No problem. Isn't it a glorious day? Have you found any bargains yet?"

"Nothing in particular," Pam said. "But to be honest I just love looking around. Car boot sales are great fun, aren't they?"

"I love them too." The girl smiled once more and then it was her turn to be served and Pam stepped away.

Standing there, feeling the warmth of the lunchtime sun on her face, Pam suddenly realised she couldn't have been happier. Which shouldn't have been that surprising really – genie or no genie, she thought ruefully – because it was exactly the state of mind she'd been in before she'd ever set eyes on Kylie or the lamp.

A WORD FROM THE AUTHOR

"This is a story about the differences between what we wish for and what – deep down – we truly want."

ILLUSTRATIONS: ALAMY, THINKSTOCK, MANDY MURRAY

On Top Of The World

With the right person by your side, the scariest things can be conquered easily… some of them even become fun!

By Tessa Ireland

Ferris wheels are something I really love!

Of course, I didn't always feel this way. No one's more afraid of heights than I am, yet on my very first ride, there I sat, swinging at the top of the wheel, *stuck* up there with two perfect strangers.

One moment I'd been standing at the foot of the wheel, congratulating myself on having two feet on the ground and the good sense to keep them there, and the next moment I'd been unceremoniously

"What's wrong, Uncle Dan?" he asked, his voice tremulous with fear.

Uncle Dan, thirtyish and tanned, reassured him, "Oh, I'm sure it's nothing much. And just look at the view from up here!" He swept his arm in a wide arc, sending the seat rocking. Twenty knuckles turned even whiter.

"Oh, sorry," he apologised over the boy's head. "I'm a linesman for the power company, and I forget that not everyone's comfortable with heights." Then, glancing meaningfully from me to the small boy, he added, "but I'm sure you're not really afraid, are you?"

He swept his arm in an arc, setting the seat rocking. My knuckles went white

hustled into a seat with an impatient "Come on, lady, move it!"

The bar clanged into place and, before I could open my mouth to protest, the seat rocked and started to rise. We sailed as far as the top, there was a shudder, and we stopped dead.

The little boy beside me, no more than five years old, was as terrified as I was. His knuckles, frozen to the bar in front of us, were as white as my own.

Taking his cue, I made a valiant effort to relax, and managed a stiff smile. "No, of course not," I lied brightly. Prying my hand off the bar, I offered him a damp palm. "I'm Amber Whitmore, Uncle Dan."

"And this is Robbie. Today is a very special day for Robbie. Any minute now, his mummy, my sister Jill, is going to present him with a new baby brother or sister. We came to the fair to try to make **Continued overleaf…**

Ferris wheels – joy
and terror mixed!

Joyous

Continued from previous page

the time go faster. Look! We can even see Mummy's hospital from here!"

"Oh, yes, I see it; I work there in Admissions. In fact, my shift starts in about an hour, so I hope we won't be stuck up here too long."

At that, Robbie's lower lip started to tremble. Anxious to make up for my gaffe, I rushed on with, "Why don't we try to find Uncle Dan's car in the car park?"

"Great idea!" agreed Dan. "Can you see it, Robbie?" He flashed me a grateful smile and took over the game. Robbie was soon fully immersed in locating familiar landmarks. It was fun, and before long we were all relaxed.

In time, Robbie actually cuddled up against Dan and succumbed to the seat's gentle rocking. The sky darkened from indigo to a velvety black as the midway lights, a mini-Vegas, blazed below. At such a height, the voices of the barkers and the music of the carousel were muted, creating a sense of isolation, perfect for quiet conversation.

My usual shyness vanished as we reminisced about our own childhood visits to the fair. Dan chuckled at my confession that my most adventurous rides had been the carousel and bumper cars, and that I really came just to indulge in the candy floss and mini-donuts.

Then, more serious, he added, "But right now, I just wish that phone would ring with some news."

He pulled it out of his pocket and glared at it. As if on cue, rock music filled the air. He flipped it open and listened intently. A relieved grin spread slowly across his face and he gave me a thumbs-up.

Suddenly there was activity below us. Our seat jerked and started to descend.

Isn't it wonderful?

My usual shyness vanished as we reminisced

Just a year after that night at the top of the wheel, Dan proposed to me – on the Ferris wheel, of course. Since then, we've never missed the annual fair – and a spin on my favourite attraction.

There's a young man in the seat below us, his arm around his girl. It's Rob, our nephew ("Aunt Amber, I'm eighteen; you can't call me Robbie any more!").

And the three little girls in the seat above? One is Rob's little sister, born the day Dan and I met, and our own two beautiful daughters.

Like I said… aren't Ferris wheels simply wonderful?

A WORD FROM THE AUTHOR

"For me, Ferris wheels have always epitomised a combination of romance tinged with sheer terror. Add a little serendipity to the mix and anything is possible!"

ILLUSTRATIONS: JAMES DEWAR, THINKSTOCK

Fancy That!

Midsummer facts that make you go "**Wow**!"

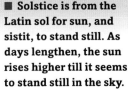

- The Druids' Solstice was the wedding of Heaven and Earth, hence the present-day belief of lucky June weddings.

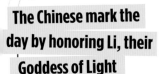

The Chinese mark the day by honoring Li, their Goddess of Light

- **June's full moon is the Honey Moon. Mead made from honey was drunk at weddings – the origin of our word honeymoon.**

- Dates for the solstice vary as the 365-day human calendar year and the 365.24-day astronomical year don't match!

- **Solstice is from the Latin sol for sun, and sistit, to stand still. As days lengthen, the sun rises higher till it seems to stand still in the sky.**

- There are magic moments in New York when the sun sets in exact alignment with the Manhattan grid, lighting every cross-street at the end of the day.

- **If you can't sleep during the Summer Solstice, sit in the middle of a stone circle and you'll see fairies and goblins!**

Summer solstice coincided with the rising of the Nile. As it was crucial to predict this annual flooding, the Egyptian New Year began on this important date

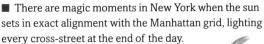

Ancient Pagans celebrated Midsummer with couples leaping over bonfires, believing their crops would grow as high as they were able to jump

Today thousands still gather at Stonehenge to welcome the sunrise on the Summer Solstice

This Summer Will Be Different

Haunted by loss, brave Ruth finds tremendous strength of character, allowing her to face the future with a smile again

By Tess Niland Kimber

Tentatively, Ruth sipped her orange juice as she stared out of the lounge window across Wheeler's Bay.

Early morning sun skittered light like diamond chips across the wide, blue sea. Eager to start the day, a red fishing boat bounced over the waves, playing a nautical game of chase with a gleaming, white yacht with number 47 painted on its sail. In a wide arc, a jet skier zoomed along, drawing a watery bracket around each boats' path.

It was a scene Ruth hadn't felt comfortable gazing on for a long while. Even now a tingle of fear shivered through her and she fought to suppress it, just as Don had told her to. Taking a deep breath, she concentrated on the sight of others happy in the July sun.

"Remember, this summer will be different…"

For a brief moment, she closed her eyes, mentally rewinding. She was safe, she told herself, with the day spread before her. Don's words echoed. She mustn't forget, she was in control.

Opening her eyes, she saw a cormorant tailing the boats. Was it Frank's? She hoped so, feeling close to him again.

Lost in the scenery, she smiled. Her cottage sat on top of cliffs, shadowing Wheeler's Bay. Whatever the season there was always the changing seascape to watch.

The beach, as golden as syrup, was spread to her left and curling round the bay in front of her was the grey-veined face of the cliffs. Grass, as thick as velvet, iced their crown and a monument to Wheeler's Bay's most famous poet pointed to the sky, warning the summer season ahead to be perfect.

"So," Andrea said, coming up behind her. "It's today."

Ruth flinched at her daughter's words. Playing for time, she said, "Today?"

The familiar fear sent a tiny trickle of sweat river-ing down her spine.

"It's the sandcastle competition, Nanny," reminded Leanne, her eleven year old grand-daughter.

"Yes," Andrea said, patiently. "You agreed you'd go."

A smile danced across Andrea's lips but there was a hint of steel in her eyes. She'd inherited Frank's blue eyes but sometimes they lacked his warmth.

A natural organiser, Ruth had relied on her husband from the moment they'd met, down there on the beach at Wheeler's Bay. He'd taken care of her,

She could see
the bay from
her window

He'd dealt with the business side of their marriage and left her all the fun things

their finances, booked their holidays, even chosen the car they drove, although he'd always let her pick the colour.

"You've got a better eye for that sort of thing," he'd praised.

Yes, he'd dealt with the business side of their marriage and left her all the fun things. Choosing the décor for their home here at Cliff Top Cottage, looking after **Continued overleaf…**

Continued from previous page

the children when they arrived and deciding where they'd go on holiday.

They made a good team …

No, Ruth thought, tears pricking her eyes now. *They* had *made a good team.*

Why couldn't she get used to it? It was two years now since Frank had died. Two years since she'd really had anyone to lean on.

"That's part of the problem, Ruth. Frank ran the family so when he died suddenly you'd too much to contend with. The shock of his death, dealing with your grief, and taking over his role. No wonder you became ill," her therapist Don had said.

"Other partners who've been left behind – are they like this?"

"In different ways, yes." He'd nodded. "Men especially. Often their wives ran their homes for decades like well-ordered ships – cooking, cleaning, shopping. Suddenly they can't cope with day-to-day life. One of my patients went to the laundrette each day because he didn't know how to turn on the washing machine."

The laundrette… for the briefest moment, Ruth envied that man.

Yes, Don's words during that session had made her feel better. But that was only the start. The mountain she'd scaled since, dwarfed Everest.

Oh, both Jeff – her son – and Andrea did their best. In fact, Ruth's daughter would happily have inherited Frank's role but, although well-meaning, she could be bossy. Not what Ruth needed. Especially when she was ill.

And now Andrea was pushing her again. Today…

Of course, she'd known. How could she forget? The date, and all it meant, was burned on her mind.

Ruth's illness had been so sudden. She supposed it was triggered by the shock of the phone call.

"Ruth? It's Terry…"

"Oh, hello, how are you?"

He'd cut her off. Telling her… She couldn't really take in his words, as if he was speaking a new language, but she registered his tone – knowing something was most awfully wrong.

The cold had started to shiver through her then – and it hadn't stopped for almost two years.

Terry's news was unbelievable. Frank had collapsed on the golf course during their game.

"A heart attack," he'd said, in this new frightening language.

She'd rushed to the hospital. Sitting beside him, she'd clutched his hand, watching as the life slipped out of him – as the light of hers followed.

Eventually the children had arrived. In a blur, they'd led her from the hospital and it was then that it first happened.

As the automatic exit doors whooshed open, she'd frozen.

"Mum… I'm parked over there," Jeff had said, cupping her elbow.

She'd started to shake violently and as they'd walked to his waiting car, she'd felt wave after wave of nausea, the ground seeming to tilt around her.

"That's half the battle, so you will, Ruth, when you're ready. It might not be this summer. Or Christmas. But one day, I promise."

So last summer, she'd stood patiently at the lounge window, watching the tourists far below playing on the beach, swimming, even surfing, while she re-lived that distant summer when she'd first met Frank.

How she'd longed to go down to

How she'd longed to go down to the bay and wander among the rock pools

"It's the shock," Andrea had said. "It's only natural."

And, for a while, she'd accepted that.

But when, a week after the funeral, she was still struggling, she knew there was more to it.

Andrea made a doctor's appointment but she couldn't go. The pattern continued, and Frank's funeral became the last day Ruth went outside.

Jeff had found Don and arranged for Ruth to see him. At home, at first. It helped so much to talk things through. Slowly, she began to think the unimaginable. That, one day – when she was ready – she might go outside again.

Last summer had been the hardest.

It had been glorious. Record temperatures and plenty going on for the visitors around Wheeler's Bay, but Ruth had missed it all.

"I feel trapped but I can't help it. Every time I go outside, I feel the same rising panic. Shaking. Nausea. I'm cross with myself. I'm letting everyone down. I do try, but I just… can't."

"You want to do this," Don had said.

Wheeler's Bay and walk among the rock pools, imagining she was hand-in-hand with him once more. But she couldn't. So she'd stood, watching and shaking and wondering whether life would ever be the same again.

It had been young Leanne who had finally forced the issue.

"It's Wheeler Bay's Sandcastle Competition next week. I want to win it – for Grandad."

Ruth was touched beyond words.

"He'd have loved that," she'd sniffed.

"He said –" Leanne pushed her blonde hair out of her eyes – "it was how you met each other."

"That's right. We were your age. My castle beat his and he never forgave me."

They'd both been wildly competitive but her Princess Castle, decorated with coloured shells, had beaten his Fort. Technically, his was better but she'd had the artistic edge.

"Even in those days you were good with colour," he'd often joked.

The competition was a bit of fun

Continued overleaf…

woven into Wheeler's Bay holiday traditions like the annual carnival and end-of-season firework display.

Since she was tiny, Leanne had entered every year, watched by her delighted grandparents, but both Frank and Ruth had been missing last year. Andrea had used the camera on her mobile phone to capture every angle, but it wasn't the same.

"Maybe next summer will be different…" she'd said.

After months of therapy, Ruth began to improve. Just after New Year she'd ventured into the garden. Walking through the open back door, she'd felt icy with fear but stepping onto the garden path had filled her with elation.

"You did it!" Don had said, proudly.

After that, there was a trip in the car. Only as far as the end of the lane, but it was a start.

Each week, she'd no sooner managed one step than another, slightly more challenging, was suggested. Sometimes, the panic was too strong and she'd retreat. But that just made her more determined. She hardly noticed how far she'd come until last week Jeff took her to the supermarket.

At first, the rush of people around her

and I'm not ready for that."

She tried to forget the crowds and concentrate on the few items of shopping she wanted to buy.

"Well done, Mum. I'm so proud of you," Jeff said as they came through the checkout and headed for the car park.

"I'm glad it's over," she said as he hugged her. "But I did it. I actually did it."

"Think what you'll do soon," he encouraged. "Go for walks in the sun, drive over to see us on Saturdays."

"I missed all of last summer," she said. "No strolls along the shore or climbing up the Downs to the statue."

He'd squeezed her hand. "You just wait, Mum. This summer will be different…"

But there was just one last hurdle to face. To be in a crowded environment, outside. Ruth's heart pounded and her hands were wet with sweat. She really didn't think she could face it.

"I don't know, Andrea. Maybe it's a bit soon. I don't want to push it. Undo all my good work."

Tears slipped down her cheeks and she braced herself for one of Andrea's "no-nonsense-now" chats.

"Nanny might not come. She's not feeling… well," her daughter excused

had been almost too much but she'd stuck it out, remembering all that Don had taught her.

"Do you want to go home?" Jeff had asked, his face pale with anxiety.

"No – I'll do it. If I let this beat me, I might as well shut myself away in Cliff Top Cottage for the rest of my life –

But instead her daughter slipped her hand in hers, just as she used to all those years ago when she'd walked her home from school.

"I know you're scared, Mum. But all that hard work – well, it just proves what you can do. It's a glorious day. There'll be lots to see. You won't have time to be

"Oh, but you promised! You said, this summer will be different."

Andrea crouched in front of Leanne. "Some promises are hard to keep."

"But it won't be the same without you…" Leanne looked up at Ruth, her blue eyes filling with tears.

Ruth bit her lip. "Okay. I'll… I'll… come."

T he beach was heaving. Sunbathers stretched out on multicoloured towels and the smell of burgers and candy floss, from the kiosk by the steps, filled the air.

The sun was burning and for a moment, Ruth was almost overcome by the simple pleasure of feeling hot sand pushing between her bare toes.

On the slipway was a man with a megaphone who soon called for everyone's attention.

"On the count of three, I want the entrants to start building their castles. When I blow the whistle, everyone must stop. The judges' decision will be final. Three – two – one! Go!"

Immediately, there was a frenzy of digging and patting.

Ruth tried to concentrate on Leanne's efforts but it was hard. Even with the crowd watching the competition, the beach felt too open, too wide. She glanced towards the sea and for a moment, the horizon seemed to tilt. Feeling the rising terror, she took a deep breath. Oh no! Don't say she was going to have another panic attack.

But Don's words filled her head as she remembered his advice.

"I can't promise you'll never feel the fear again but I can teach you to cope with it. You're in control. Not your fear."
Continued overleaf…

nervous. And besides, it's the sandcastle competition."

"Where I met your father."

"Yes. It brought you luck all those years ago, didn't it?"

Ruth smiled through her tears. "You're right… But what if I have a wobble?"

"Then I'll bring you right back home."

"Oh, I don't know. It's too soon. Too far. Too busy…"

Just then the lounge door opened and Leanne skipped in wearing a white t-shirt and yellow shorts. Quickly, Ruth wiped away her tears.

"Nanny – are you crying?"

"No, of course not." She blew her nose and forced a smile. "Touch of hay fever, that's all."

"Good. It's the competition today. I want you to cheer me on. You missed it last year and next summer, I'll be too old to enter."

"Nanny might not come. She's not feeling… well," Andrea said.

Continued from previous page

She took a deep breath and watched as the horizon levelled. A cormorant flew overhead, screeching as if it was having as much fun as the battling children.

Was it Frank's?

"All right, Mum," Andrea asked, concern haunting her eyes.

"Yes. I think so."

Squeezing her hands together, she turned back to watch Leanne build her castle, her blonde head bent over in concentration. Was that how she'd appeared to Frank, all those years ago?

When the whistle blew, the judges solemnly walked between the castles, marking each entry on their clipboards.

Then the compere spoke again.

She watched the cormorant float on the breeze and felt a closeness to Frank

"In first place – Matthew Shiner…"

Ruth felt the sear of her granddaughter's disappointment.

"And in a close second place, we've Leanne Latter with her Magical Castle."

When Leanne jumped up and yelled, "Yay!" both Andrea and Ruth laughed.

"She's a good loser – better than her grandfather." Ruth smiled.

"At least, I'll get my name on the cup," Leanne said when the local press photographer had finished taking her picture with the castle.

Without telling anyone what she planned and after they'd all gone home, Ruth quietly slipped down to the near-empty beach again.

Sitting on the shore, she watched the peachy sun slide out of the sky. Tears fell down her cheeks as she thought over and over, *I've done it. I've got my life back.*

A cormorant – was it the one from this afternoon; the one she liked to think was Frank's? – squawked overhead.

She watched it float on the breeze above her for a moment, feeling that same closeness to him.

"Yes, you're right," she breathed. "This summer will be different…"

And now, finally, she truly believed that it would.

A WORD FROM THE AUTHOR

"I live on the gorgeous Isle of Wight. After reading an article in My Weekly about agoraphobia, I felt sad for sufferers 'imprisoned' by this condition, unable to enjoy our lovely summers."

Secrets In The City

How is Mandy ever going to meet someone when she hates the noisy clubs her sociable friend adores?

Continued overleaf…

By Wendy Kremer

Cradling her mug of coffee, Mandy peeked through to the sitting room. Her friend and flatmate Gill was dancing to some music blaring out of the radio. Watching her friend's uninhibited movements through serious green eyes, Mandy smiled wistfully, wishing silently that she could sometimes be as outgoing and unrestrained – but then, a leopard couldn't change its spots.

Gill was always on a never-ending round of parties and celebrations; her phone never stopped ringing. Mandy picked up her friend's empty mug and ducked past her on the way to the tiny kitchen. Neatly, she swilled out the mugs and turned them upside down on the draining board.

Mandy looked at her watch. She just had time to get to the library to change her books before it closed. She collected the pile of finished novels from her bedside table, donned her coat and lifted the books to show Gill where she was

woman move towards the shelves and wondered why such a pretty girl had so much spare time for reading. At that age, she'd been painting the town red.

With a new stack under her arm, Mandy retraced her steps. She bounded up the stairs and after depositing the books in her bedroom, she knocked on the bathroom door where Gill was clearly busy titivating herself. "I'm back. Are you in or out tonight? I'm going to make some macaroni cheese – want some?"

Gill's voice was muffled by the door and the steam. "No thanks, love. There's a party down the docks tonight. Grant will be picking me up in an hour. Why don't you come with us?"

Mandy mused that, different as they were, Gill was a great friend to her. She led a hectic social life by any standard, but she always tried to include Mandy in her activities. Now and then Mandy had given in and gone with her, but it wasn't her kind of world and she'd never felt happy among flashing lights, dark

"You're staying in on a Friday night?" he asked incredulously. "Are you ill?"

going before she left. Gill nodded and continued shimmying and twirling.

Outside, Mandy enjoyed the fresh headiness of a beautiful spring day. Her step lightened as she walked quickly down the High Street towards the small library. She was a regular borrower and they knew her well.

"Hi, Mandy, a couple of new historicals just arrived! The one that was praised sky-high by the critics is still over there… on that extra gantry."

Maureen Turner watched the young

surroundings and ear-splitting music.

Shaking her head at the closed door, and breathing in the smell of some exotic bath essence swirling towards her through the cracks, Mandy shouted back. "No, thanks. Do you want some macaroni, or not?"

There was a muffled "No thanks" from within, and then

the sound of a body and water swirling around in the bathtub.

When he arrived, Grant was dressed in a blue designer suit. The jacket looked as if he'd slept in it, but Mandy could guess it was expensive and the latest style, so she didn't comment. Waiting for Gill to collect the thousands of things she stuffed in her handbag every time she went out, Grant eyed her and asked, "So, where are you going then?"

Folding her arms tightly in front of her, Mandy mumbled, "Nowhere."

Grant looked incredulous. "Nowhere? You're staying in on a Friday evening? Are you ill?"

"No, I'm fine."

His eyes swept over her. "You're not bad looking, either. Take my advice – don't waste your time. Life is too short."

Blushing slightly, Mandy tried to smile.

"We all have different ideas about having fun. Gill and I are different."

"You can say that again. She doesn't slow down for a second; it's like being attached to the end of a rocket. While you seem to be nailed to the ground, if you don't mind me saying so."

Mandy did mind – she minded a lot – but she shook her head dismissively.

"We can't all be live-wires."

Taking in the serious expression on her face and her muted clothes, he answered callously, "Live wire? It looks as if your fuse went out before anyone even lit it." He laughed loudly at his own joke.

Mandy was hurt, although she strove not to show it. She was glad when Gill waltzed into the room, still pushing things into her bag and trailing a coat behind her. "Okay, let's go, Grant. We're **Continued overleaf…**

already late. Night, then, Mandy!"

"Night!" Mandy watched them leave. The flat seemed terribly silent, and she still felt miffed and offended. She might not be a dancing queen, but she was doing what she wanted to; she had a good job, a loving family and was liked by the people who knew her well. Who needed to be centre stage all the time?

Mandy enjoyed a comforting plateful of macaroni and washed up. The kitchen was tidy, so was her bedroom and she'd also tidied the bathroom after Gill. She shut the door on Gill's bedroom firmly; it looked as if it had been targeted by a hurricane. And now Mandy was looking forward to reading to her heart's content… or was she?

Grant's thoughtless remarks had jolted her self-confidence. She'd finished with her last real boyfriend over a year ago; someone she'd liked, but who'd never managed to bring her any excitement.

The trilling phone interrupted any further deliberations.

"Hello!" There was a moment's pause. "Is that Gill?"

Mandy felt exasperated; yet another boyfriend. Why couldn't it be for her for once? Daggers drawn, she returned, "Yes – who's that?"

"Paul… You sound strange!"

"Do I? I've got a cold. I probably do sound a bit funny."

"You do. Hope you're better soon. I just wanted to remind you about the shindig on Sunday. You're still coming?"

"Sunday?" she repeated.

'Yeah, at the Golden Goose – formal suit and tie, remember?"

Trying to sound nonchalant and Gill-like, she replied hastily, "Oh yes. Almost forgot! Thanks for the reminder."

"Okay. I'll see you there, seven-thirty?"

"Yes, okay. Seven-thirty it is."

Mandy liked the sound of his voice; it was deep and friendly. She didn't understand why, but for the first time in her life, she'd deliberately lied to a stranger on the phone – to one of Gill's boyfriends. Some devil was tempting her to be daring.

The message she'd written on the page danced around before her eyes as she wondered and speculated about whether she should tell Gill after all, or turn up in her stead and make up an excuse about why Gill couldn't come. If it was a formal get-together, it meant she could wear the sort of clothes she liked wearing anyway.

The idea excited her. It wasn't sensible, but something drove her on; perhaps Grant's facetious remarks had spurred her into action. Or perhaps she just needed a little adventure in her life at this moment.

Gill was curious when Mandy announced she had a date on Sunday; she was vague about it and Gill gathered he was someone Mandy didn't know very well.

Eyeing her friend over the top of her book, Mandy felt increasingly uncomfortable. What if Gill found out that Mandy had pinched her boyfriend? They'd always been the best of friends, despite the fact they were like chalk and cheese. She knew nothing about Paul. He could be Gill's casual boyfriend, someone to send me such an attractive replacement. This is a dinner given by my boss and it's important for me to make the right impression." He considered her smart two-piece outfit with its shaped jacket, her high heels, her intelligent face and gentle green eyes. "I must say, she's come out tops!"

Mandy coloured slightly and remained silent, glancing up at him.

"Shall we go in?"

Mandy nodded and fell into step alongside him. The tables were already almost fully occupied so Paul didn't have much trouble finding their places.

The evening was a success; for Paul,

Several times his glance met hers and hesitated. She stepped towards him

she was serious about, or even her love of a lifetime. Mandy didn't feel so happy about meeting him any more – but she'd gone too far to turn back.

In the lobby of the Golden Goose, she rid herself of her coat and looked around the crowd of people, waiting. Paul would be expecting to meet Gill – not her. Gradually the room emptied, and there were only a handful of middle-aged people and one young man left. He was tall and rangy with brown hair that flopped onto his forehead and reached his collar. He had dark eyes, and they were busily searching the room. Several times his glance met hers and hesitated for a fraction of a second before moving on. Mandy swallowed the lump in her throat and approached him.

"Paul?" He nodded. "I'm afraid Gill couldn't come. She asked me to step in for her. I'm Mandy."

He smiled. "Hello, Mandy. Good of Gill

his boss and for Mandy. She'd never felt so at home with anyone as quickly as she did with Paul. In between the speeches and conversations with some of his workmates, the two of them discovered that they liked the same films, the same books and loved visiting museums and art exhibitions. It seemed natural to tell him how she loved walking along the seashore, and how she'd always wanted to fly in a helicopter. By the end of the evening, she really felt as if she'd known him all her life.

Later he walked her back to her car and held out his hand.

"Thanks for coming. My boss was impressed – and you saved my bacon."

His hand was warm and firm and she didn't want to let go. "My pleasure. I enjoyed myself, honestly."

"Perhaps… perhaps we can meet again? There's an exhibition in the Town **Continued overleaf…**

Hall next weekend. Modern paintings by someone I've never heard of, but we could take a look round and then have a cup of coffee together?"

She beamed. "I'd like that very much."

"Good!" He smiled too. He leaned down and softly kissed her cheek, before she turned away from him in confusion and scrambled into her Mini.

After several heavenly dates with Paul, guilt was beginning to eat into Mandy's soul. Gill pumped her for information about the new boyfriend and it was getting more difficult to evade all the questions. Mandy found it terribly hard to be vague and elusive.

Gill was her best friend, and Mandy was developing stomach ache every time Gill mentioned the word *boyfriend*. She sometimes told fibs about where she was going so that Gill wouldn't know she was meeting Paul again, and she could tell

Gill was painting her toenails a bright scarlet; she looked up, pleased. "Yes! I'd love to, Mandy."

"Good." Mandy trailed off to her room feeling the weight of the world on her shoulders. She phoned Paul.

"I'm bringing my best friend along with me tomorrow. You don't mind, do you?"

His voice was amused. "I'd rather have you all to myself, but of course I don't mind. You sound a bit bothered, though. Anything wrong?"

"No, I hope not."

"You hope not? That doesn't sound very encouraging."

"I'll explain tomorrow. Night!"

Surprised by the abruptness of her tone, Paul just repeated "Night!" and wondered exactly what was wrong.

The sky was overcast. The clouds were a dismal grey and there was an uncomfortable wind pulling at their coats

"If neither of you ever want to see me again, I understand completely…"

that Gill was getting very suspicious.

Mandy couldn't ask Gill any questions about Paul, either – she might click.

After a couple of weeks, Mandy decided she'd have to come out into the open. She couldn't keep lying to Gill, or to Paul. There was a lump in her throat at the thought that Paul and her best friend might both hate her for what she'd done.

She and Paul arranged to meet the following evening. Mandy decided it was time to be honest, even if she lost him; she had to be candid.

"Gill, would you like to meet my friend? We're meeting down at the wine bar tomorrow evening. Coming?"

as Mandy, with Gill in tow, reached the pub. She wondered with a pang whether she'd ever come here again after today; it was their favourite pub.

Paul was sitting at a corner table in the semi-darkness as she went towards him. Gill was her shadow, and Mandy drew a deep breath before she moved aside and sat down, leaving Gill and Paul facing each other across the table.

Gill was clearly startled. "What… what are *you* doing here?"

Paul seemed stunned – though not by Gill's tight leather trousers and pink leopard print top. "I could ask you the same thing," he returned.

They turned in unison to face a very pale Mandy. Almost in unison, they asked, "What's this all about?"

Mandy looked down, gathering the courage to face them again. She concentrated on Paul's face because she loved him the most.

"I… I'm so sorry!"

"Sorry? What about?"

"When you called to remind Gill about meeting you at the Golden Goose, it was me on the phone. I never told Gill you'd phoned, and I decided to come as her replacement. That's who I told you I was – Gill's replacement. After we'd met and went on meeting, I didn't know how to tell you the truth any more. I know you're entitled to be mad, and I'm really sorry if I've come between you. I can't go on without you knowing the truth." Her face crumpled. "And if you never want to see me again, I understand completely."

Gill and Paul exchanged astonished looks, and then burst into laughter.

Mandy felt annoyed. "It's nothing to laugh about. Don't laugh at me, please."

Paul slid across the leather seat and put his arm round her shoulder. "Oh, Mandy! We're not laughing at you. We're laughing at fate. Aren't we, Gill?"

Gill nodded, wiping her eyes. "Heavens, Mandy – I was really worried about this mysterious man of yours. I couldn't get any information out of you however I tried, and I was scared in case some weirdo had you under his control."

Mandy looked at her in amazement. "You're not mad about me meeting Paul, instead of you?"

Her friend laughed again. "I ought to be, but I'm not. Of course I'm not."

"But Paul is…"

"Paul is my cousin, you twerp! If you take a proper look at him, you can see the resemblance – and you ought to realise he's not my idea of a boyfriend. Do you honestly believe I'd be interested in someone who likes made-to-measure suits, polo shirts, tweed jackets, chinos and brogues? Perhaps he sets your pulse racing and he may be a great bloke, but he's much too quiet for my taste." She gave a peal of laughter.

Mandy felt the load lift from her heart. She coloured. "I'm sorry for not being truthful – it'll never happen again."

Paul gave her a hug and Gill said, "Silly old twerp! How about getting us something to drink, Paul? Something to celebrate. Mandy's out on the town!"

A WORD FROM THE AUTHOR

"I'm a hopeless chocolate addict, cat owner, mother, and ex-patriate now living in Germany. This particular story was inspired by observing people and how they sometimes act and react."

Within The Crystal Ball

We may catch glimpses of the future – but do we have the understanding to interpret what we're being shown…?

By Sandra Lynn

Cheryl is my best friend and next-door neighbour and we have loved browsing around charity shops together ever since we moved into the same street five years ago. We call it our budget version of retail therapy and we often manage to pick up some great treasures and bargains without breaking our budgets. Of course, we blow most of the money we save on cappuccino and cheesecake, but it makes for a great day out.

Our husbands don't mind either, though they always shake their heads when we bring home a new box of goodies and they pretend we've spent a fortune. My Tim was really thrilled with the 1987 signed and framed Grand Final team photo I picked up for only fifty pence and immediately hung it up on the wall in his office.

Cheryl's hubby Greg loved the carved wooden chess set we found at one garage sale, even though it was missing one of the pawns. One day he's going to learn to play chess, but for now it looks great on the mantelpiece.

We collected all sorts of interesting and sometimes useful things, but my favourite object d'art was an old crystal ball I found covered in dust in the corner of a bric-a-brac store. The owner seemed glad to get rid of it and only charged me five pounds. He said it came from an eccentric old lady whose family had decided she needed nursing home care.

"She claimed she could see things in it," he said, "but she was just… you know…" He pointed to his head while making a circular motion, implying the

I found a crystal ball, covered in dust, in the corner of a quirky bric-a-brac store

old lady was crazy. I pressed him for more details but he just shook his head. I could have beaten him down more on the price, but Cheryl had gone on ahead to the coffee shop to order our cappuccinos and cheesecake, so I left with my prize safely wrapped in lots of newspaper.

Cheryl said it gave her the creeps and Tim wouldn't let me display it in the lounge, so I set it up in the spare room I

used for sewing and storage. I thought it looked great on its wooden stand once I gave it a good clean.

I tried looking into it but I couldn't see anything, except when the late afternoon sun shone through the window and it deflected a magnificent rainbow light across the ceiling.

One day we decided to hold our own garage sale and as well as cleaning out our cupboards we thought it was about time we let go of some of the bargains we realised we really didn't need after all.

Out went three dinner sets, six vases, a **Continued overleaf…**

chipped Wedgwood plate, a birdcage, twenty-two sets of novelty salt-and-pepper shakers, and jeans that I had to concede I was never ever going to fit into.

"Why don't you get rid of that creepy crystal ball?" suggested Tim, so reluctantly I put it out on the table, too.

The jeans went to a lady who was certain she would be able to fit them if she stuck to her diet and most of the other items found new owners, but no one was interested in my crystal ball, not even when I reduced the price and practically gave it away.

I was secretly glad and at the end of the day took it back to the sewing room while Tim, Cheryl and Greg added up our takings. I was standing back to admire it

I nearly choked, spluttering my red wine all down the front of my blouse. I quickly regained my composure and congratulated Cheryl and Greg. I knew they had been trying for a baby for almost a year and I was thrilled for them – but the vision in the crystal ball had me spooked. I kissed them both and excused myself to go and change my blouse.

"I'm really sorry," I heard Cheryl telling Tim, "I hope our news didn't upset her. I didn't realise you two were trying for a baby, too."

Tim hastened to assure Cheryl that we weren't planning the pitter patter of little feet just yet but I noticed she looked at me quizzically several times during the evening as we ate our pizza and watched

I peered closer and saw the image of a newborn baby in the cloudy crystal ball

on the shelf when I noticed strange shadows appearing to move around inside the suddenly cloudy ball. I peered closer and saw the image of a newborn baby in a cradle. I opened my mouth to call the others but quickly thought better of it. I wasn't sure how they'd react.

A little shaken, I made my way out to join the others in the kitchen. "We thought we'd order pizza," said Tim, and I readily agreed. We had made a tidy sum with our garage sale, including a nice profit on some of our junk shop gems.

"And let's have a drop of this red," suggested Tim after he rang the pizza shop. He pulled a bottle out from the rickety wine rack I had bought for only two pounds a few months previously.

"Umm… none for me." Cheryl stammered and grinned at her husband. "We've got some news. I'm pregnant!"

an old movie. I smiled back but I found it hard to look her in the eye.

I didn't dare tell Tim or Cheryl about what I had seen in the crystal ball as I was sure they would think I was crazy. I told myself that I must have been tired and imagined the whole thing, but every day I went back into the spare room and peered into it. It remained clear.

I was really happy for Cheryl and Greg and our expeditions around the charity shops became even more fun as we hunted for baby gear. Cheryl soon found a beautiful wooden cradle that only needed a fresh coat of paint and I presented her with a soft, fluffy teddy bear, still in its original packaging.

I assured Cheryl that I was fine with her having a baby and it was the truth. Tim and I had decided to wait until the following year, after we had a chance to save a bit more and update our old car. She seemed satisfied with my excuse that my mishap with the wine was simply a case of being too tired combined with the surprise news.

Six months later we invited Cheryl and Greg over for a barbecue to celebrate her thirtieth birthday. Despite her awkward condition, Cheryl was jumping with excitement.

"Look what Greg bought for my birthday!" she gushed and pointed to their driveway adjoining ours. There stood a shiny new red car with personalised number plates. Cheryl and Greg had saved hard and I was happy for my friend even though it made our car look worse than ever.

I excused myself and went into the sewing room to fetch the birthday present I had hidden there for Cheryl. As I picked it up I noticed the crystal ball had turned cloudy again. I peered inside the glass and saw an image of a shiny red car driving along the road… suddenly another red car crashed into it – then an angel floated up from it. In my fright I dropped the present. Fortunately, I had decided on a new cardigan instead of a china bowl. I slowly picked it up and took it out to the birthday girl.

Cheryl said she loved the cardigan but I noticed that once again she eyed me uncertainly all night. I knew I probably appeared to be acting very strangely and I longed to tell her about the crystal ball and the eerie images appearing inside it, but I was afraid she'd think I was mad – or afraid it really was showing me the future.

We had arranged to go out early the next morning and look around the garage sales, knowing we might not get as many chances once the baby was born. Armed with the newspaper and a local map we got into my car. I turned the key but it didn't respond. I tried again and again but there was no result.

"It's okay, we'll take mine," Cheryl suggested. "I'll go and get my keys."

"But you drove last week and it's supposed to be my turn," I insisted, giving the key another try. We always took it in turns as neither of us could afford the petrol.

The car still refused to start and I cursed, banging my fist on the dashboard. Cheryl offered again to use her new car but I was determined to get mine to start.

"Hey, you've been acting really weird lately," blurted Cheryl angrily. "I think you're jealous because I'm having a baby and I've got a new car!" It was most unlike Cheryl but she seemed really upset. I couldn't really blame her.

"No!" I answered and began to explain, but she wouldn't listen and got out of my car and slammed the door, waddling back across the front lawn.
Continued overleaf…

Continued from previous page

I shouldn't have but I got indignant then. How dare she accuse me of jealousy after all our years of friendship? It was nothing like that – but then she didn't know what was really bothering me. I should have gone after her but I have a terrible stubborn streak.

I went back into my kitchen to make coffee and by the time I finished I had cooled down. I realised the best thing would be to go over and explain the whole situation to Cheryl, even if she did think I was mad. I hoped we'd have a good laugh about it. But just as I opened my front door I saw Cheryl's car back out of her driveway and down the road.

said Cheryl as we went together to take a look at the crystal ball, which remained clear once again.

Then I heard another knock on my

The vision flashed before my eyes and I couldn't think of life without my friend

I waved frantically but she didn't see me – or pretended not too. I tried to call her on her mobile phone but she didn't answer, so I spent the morning pacing up and down, stopping to check her driveway every few minutes.

The vision I had seen in the crystal ball kept flashing before my eyes, I couldn't bear to think of life without my friend. I should have told her the night before.

Then at last there was a knock on my door. "I'm sorry!" we both said together.

"I think it's my hormones," said Cheryl as we hugged. "I know you're not the jealous type."

"I was partly to blame, too," I assured her and over coffee I explained about the crystal ball.

"I must have been imagining things, but it really spooked me. Thank goodness there wasn't an accident after all."

"I have to agree it's pretty spooky,"

door. I opened it to find a man dressed in a suit and carrying a clipboard. "Mrs Abby Phillips?"

"Yes, that's me," I replied.

"Congratulations! You bought a raffle ticket for the Angels Foundation last month and I'm pleased to tell you you've won a new car!"

He waved his arm toward the driveway and there, behind my old jalopy, was a shiny red car.

Teatime Treat

FUN AND FRUITY

Chocolate & Orange Cupcakes

Chocolate Orange Cupcakes

Preparation time: 35min
Cooking time: 20min
Makes 12

Ingredients

- 115g butter, softened
- 115g caster sugar
- Finely grated zest of 1 orange
- 2 eggs, beaten
- 115g self raising flour
- 1tbsp cocoa powder, sifted
- 1tbsp orange juice

For the icing:

- 115g butter, softened
- 225g icing sugar, sifted
- Finely grated zest of 1 orange
- 3tbsp orange juice
- Terry's Chocolate Orange segments

● Preheat the oven to 180°C, Fan Oven 160°C, Gas Mark 4. Line a 12-hole bun tin with cake cases.

● Cream the **butter** and **sugar** together until light and fluffy. Beat in the **orange zest**. Add the **eggs** a little at a time, beating well between each addition.

● Sift the **flour** and **cocoa powder** together into the mixture and mix in carefully. Stir in the **orange juice**. Divide the mixture up into the cake cases.

Place in the preheated oven and cook for 15-20min. Remove from the oven and allow to cool on a wire rack.

● To make the icing, beat the **butter** and **icing sugar** together until smooth, beat in the **orange zest** and **juice**. Once the cakes are cool, pipe the icing on the top and place a **Chocolate Orange segment** on top. Alternatively spread with the icing before topping with the segment.

RECIPE: FIONA BURRELL PHOTOGRAPHY: LIGHTHOUSE

The Soldier & The Statue

He was having a really bad day, until he got his chance –
after all, it is a soldier's duty to protect the gods of Rome!

By Paula Williams

As Marcus turned the corner into the main street, a blast of icy wind lifted the corner of his cloak, whipped it into his face and caught him a stinging slap in the eye.

He muttered a silent curse as water from his now streaming eye ran down his cheek and collected uncomfortably under his chin strap.

He looked quickly around him, then unfastened the strap and removed his helmet. He tucked the helmet under his arm, wiped his eye and enjoyed the sensation of the wind ruffling his hair.

back. He whirled round and found himself being glared at by a rather large woman, with a heavily laden basket.

"Watch where you go," she growled in a thick, almost unintelligible accent.

He replaced his helmet and forced himself to remember his training and what he was here for.

"I'm sorry –" he began but she shrank away from his extended hand as if he'd offered her a cup of poison.

Marcus shook his head as he watched her bustle away, still muttering crossly to herself. Then he fastened his chin strap and continued his long, lonely march along the cobbled streets, his steps – and his pulse – quickening as he approached

The soldier continued his long and lonely march along the cobbled streets

He'd be in serious trouble if he was seen on duty without the helmet, but so what? It was uncomfortable and gave him a headache. He hated the wretched thing almost as much as he hated the rest of his stupid uniform.

One of these days, he'd tell them what they could do with –

He stumbled and almost dropped his helmet as he was pushed roughly in the

the statue. He stopped and gazed up at her in awe. Minerva, the Roman goddess of wisdom and medicine – and goodness knows what else besides.

She stood, as serenely beautiful as always, on her plinth near the entrance to the Roman Baths. She had one slender arm outstretched and a thoughtful, half-smiling expression on her exquisite face.
Continued overleaf…

Remembering his training, he put on a brave face

Continued from previous page

She was, quite simply, the loveliest creature he'd ever seen. And he was head over heels in love with her. She was the last thing he thought about when he went to sleep and the first thing he thought about when he awoke next morning. She filled his every waking thought.

Of course, he could never tell her how he felt, and as for telling his mates – no way! He was a big enough laughing stock among them as it was, with his tall, gangly frame and his spindly white legs that stuck out beneath his tunic like two sticks of blanched celery. Julius Caesar he was not.

"Quick, lads, over here!" The cry came from a barrel-chested youth with a face like a bad-tempered bulldog. "Come and see what I've found. It's a little soldier boy. Look at his little matchstick legs. Did you ever seen anything quite so funny? Who does he look like?"

Marcus stiffened, his hand on the hilt of his sword as a group of seven, maybe eight, jeering youths surrounded him.

They were roughly dressed with hoods pulled low across their faces.

He watched warily as Bulldog-face came closer. There was no smile now on his heavy red face, jeering or otherwise. His eyes were cold and hostile, his posture threatening.

He made a sudden lunge but Marcus jumped aside, his heart thumping, his breathing ragged. He wished he could set about them with his sword. That would stop the lot of them in their tracks.

Only, of course, he couldn't.

"I expect you to treat everyone with courtesy," he'd been told. "No matter what the provocation. Always remember you're out there on those streets to represent the Roman Empire, which means conducting yourself well at all times. You're supposed to be the pride of Rome… even if your physique isn't quite what one expects of a Roman soldier. You're a little on the thin side, to say the least, but never mind. Just be friendly and approachable and don't respond to insults. They go with the job, I'm afraid."

That was the warning – his final, final warning, he'd been assured – that he'd received yesterday after an encounter with another group of youths had ended with him losing his cloak to them after a bit of a tussle.

They were a different group today but with the same stupid comments, the same delight in baiting him.

Today he'd been begrudgingly handed another, much inferior, cloak and warned again that this was his last chance. Any more trouble or losses and he'd be assigned kitchen duties instead.

That would be disastrous because it meant he wouldn't see Minerva. She was the only bright spot in his otherwise

he was going to stand by while they insulted his precious Minerva. And if they laid so much as one grubby finger on her, so help him he'd –

A scream pierced the air. Then yells and shrieks of jeering laughter. Marcus couldn't see what was going on because a large crowd, attracted by the noise, had gathered around the statue.

He elbowed his way through, frantic to put himself between Minerva and the gang. This was all his fault. If he hadn't walked away from them, they wouldn't have gone after another, even softer target. He reached Minerva and looked up, expecting the worst – but she was still on her plinth, smiling down on everyone,

Marcus drew his sword and ran towards them, his eyes blazing with anger

miserable day. How would he bear it if he couldn't see her any more? He pulled his cloak tightly around him, then turned and walked away from the youths, their jeering laughter ringing in his ears.

But his relief when they didn't follow him was short-lived.

"What sort of work of art do you think that is, then?" he heard Bulldog-face ask, to a chorus of catcalls from his mates. "I thought them Romans liked their statues nude. This one's got her clothes on. Still, you can see she's got nice –"

"Keep your hands off her, you moron!" Marcus shouted as he drew his sword and ran towards them, his eyes blazing. He'd take all the insults they could heap on him, but there was no way

as serenely as ever.

"You're too late, mate. They've scarpered," an old lady cackled. "The whole lot of them. You've never seen anything so funny in your life. They took off like all the hounds of hell were on their heels."

Up on her plinth "Minerva" was enjoying the sound of coins chinking in the tray at her feet. Judging from the size of the crowd that had gathered around, there should be quite a tidy sum in there by now, she reckoned.

Her arm ached, she had an itch on the end of her nose and she'd be really glad when her stint was over and she could get down and stretch her cramped limbs.

People teased her that it was easy money being paid to stand around doing nothing all day but it was really hard work **Continued overleaf…**

Continued from previous page

holding the same pose for so long.

But she wasn't complaining. Being a Living Statue was one of the best holiday jobs she'd ever had, and so much better than waitressing. The money was okay and it was such fun fooling tourists of all nationalities that thronged the entrance to the city's world famous Roman Baths – tourists who assumed she was just another statue.

As for that foul-mouthed young tearaway just now, he'd been so busy showing off to his mates, he hadn't realised she wasn't made of stone at all, just cleverly dressed and made up to look almost like it.

His shocked scream as her hand had

Minerva was as poised as ever

There was no way he was going to just stand by while they insulted Minerva

suddenly snaked out and grabbed him by the wrist had just the effect she'd hoped for. And, as an added bonus, it had brought the tourists flocking towards her like a crowd of seagulls after a fishing boat, cameras clicking, coins chinking.

It had also brought the young soldier running, she'd noticed. Funny thing, when he'd first appeared in the square, she thought he looked really silly in that Roman soldier get-up as he handed out flyers advertising a newly opened Italian restaurant called The Roman Empire.

He was tall and gangly and didn't really have the legs for strutting around in a skimpy Roman tunic.

But today, when she saw how he'd faced up to that gang and refused to let them rile him, then how quick he was to come and defend her when he thought she was being bothered by them, she'd

begun to see him in a different light and realised that, underneath that helmet, he really was quite good-looking.

So maybe, when she finished work this afternoon, she'd suggest that they have a coffee together. But only, of course, if he didn't mind waiting while she took all this make-up and stuff off – and, of course, provided he, too, promised to change.

There was no way she was going into a coffee shop with a guy wearing a skirt that was shorter than hers.

A WORD FROM THE AUTHOR

"I'm lucky to live near the beautiful city of Bath, where the sight of an unhappy young man wandering about in a skimpy Roman costume got me thinking..."

Teatime Treat

NO BAKING!

Honeycomb Sweetie Cake

Ingredients
- 150g unsalted butter
- 450g milk chocolate, broken into chunks
- 150g Malted Milk biscuits, crushed into small pieces
- 100g sultanas
- 75g mini marshmallows
- 150g honeycomb, lightly crushed
- Hundreds and thousands, to decorate tops of cakes

VERY EASY TO MAKE

Preparation time: 20min plus cooling and chilling
Cooking time: 5min
Makes 36

- Line a 20cm square cake tin with cling film. Put **butter** and **milk chocolate** in a saucepan over a very low heat to melt. Stir occasionally, then set aside to cool for 10min. Meanwhile, put **biscuits**, **sultanas** and **mini marshmallows** in a bowl, and stir in the **honeycomb**.
- Spoon the **melted chocolate** **mixture** over the **dry ingredients** and mix well to thoroughly coat everything. Pile into prepared tin and press down well. Sprinkle with **hundreds and thousands**. Cover loosely and chill for about 2hr until firm and set.
- To serve, carefully remove the chocolate cake from the tin and discard the cling film. Using a large, sharp knife, cut in 6 thin slices one way; quarter turn and cut in 6 slices in the other direction to make 36 small cubes.

RECIPE: KATHRYN HAWKINS PHOTOGRAPHY: LIGHTHOUSE

You Are Invited. . .

Real life can be every bit as thrilling as fiction – especially when Jane's lively group of friends decide to get involved!

By Jan Snook

Jane picked up her copy of that month's book and put it in her bag, along with the crisp white envelopes. It seemed a long time since she'd been to her book group – a lifetime ago, though it was only two months. But with everything that had happened, well! And yet the last book group meeting had started it all off, in a way…

They'd been reading Jane Austen's *Persuasion,* she remembered, and she'd would all be far more literary and knowledgeable than she was, they had fast become firm friends. They remembered one another's birthdays, lent each other hats for weddings and supported one another through family crises. Not to mention swapping plant cuttings and recipes. Despite their different ages – she was the youngest at forty-two, and Hazel was nearly seventy – they all got on very well. It was hard to remember Life Before Book Group.

Jane looked round the room again. "Where's Chris?" she asked in surprise.

They'd become firm friends; it was hard to remember Life Before Book Group

arrived at Tracy's house a few minutes late. The room was already full, and the others were fishing their copies of the book out of bags, handing round photos of a new grandchild, sipping glasses of wine, searching for their specs, and, of course, talking nineteen to the dozen. The meetings were the highlight of the month for Jane: the group had started almost ten years ago, and although Jane had been terrified at first that the others

It was really unusual for any of them to miss a meeting.

"Her mother's in hospital," Tracy replied, handing her a glass of white wine. "Chris has gone to visit her this evening, because they're going away for the weekend, and she won't be able to visit then. She's hoping to get here, but she'll be a bit late."

"I've met her mother," Jane said after a moment's thought. "Perhaps I could visit

her. It's miserable having no visitors."

"Oh, would you? I'm sure that would be a weight off Chris's mind. She was feeling awful about going away and leaving her." Tracy glanced at her watch. "We really must get started: there's such a lot to say about this book. Jane, maybe you can begin. What did you think of it?"

Jane paused, wondering where to start.

"Come on Jane," Hazel encouraged, "give us your usual percipient views. You always tell us exactly how the characters feel – I only ever know what they do."

Continued overleaf…

Jane looked at her, surprised. "Well, actually, I do think I know how one of these characters felt," she began, "because Anne is rather like me." The others looked at her, enquiringly. "I mean, I've got two sisters rather like the ones in the book, and…" She hesitated, and then it all came out in a rush.

"And I used to be engaged, and broke it off rather stupidly."

The others were looking at her in

"Jane, honestly! As if we believe that!"

Jane looked at the eagerly expectant faces and rolled her eyes. "Oh all right! He was doing voluntary work in Ghana. He'd got his degree and couldn't decide what he was going to do next, I suppose. He was sort of… drifting."

"And what's he doing now, do you know?" Tracy asked breathlessly.

"That's the silly thing. While he was abroad he was so appalled at how the

"Jane, honestly! As if we believe that you've forgotten what your fiancé did"

amazement, all discussion of the book utterly forgotten.

"You've never told us that!"

"Well, it's all a long time ago. A very long time ago." She looked down. "I was an idiot. And very young."

"So what happened?"

Jane looked around at the circle of sympathetic faces. *I hadn't meant to make a big deal of this,* she thought, rather flustered. "Well, that's it, really," she finished lamely.

"No it's not! You can't leave us in limbo like this, Jane," Hazel said, "what happened?"

Jane swallowed. "Well, a friend of mine persuaded me that anyone who didn't have a proper career wasn't really husband material. Really quite old fashioned stuff – you know, if-he-really-loved-you-he'd-get-a-proper-job sort of approach."

"Just like Anne's friend in *Persuasion,* you mean. Why, what did this fiancé of yours do?"

"Oh – I can scarcely remember any details, it's so long ago."

workers were treated on some cocoa plantation that he decided to become a lawyer, and you can't say that's not a proper career. He practices round here, actually." Jane gave a weak smile. "Anyway, that's quite enough from me."

Annette opened her mouth to speak, but the front door opened at that moment, and Chris appeared, slightly out of breath, in the doorway.

"I'm so sorry I'm late – my poor mother's in quite a bad way. Really very weak and a bit wobbly. But don't let me interrupt the discussion." She accepted a drink and settled herself next to Jane.

They talked animatedly about the book for the next hour, at which point Tracy got up and went into the kitchen to make coffee and the others reverted to swapping gossip, and covertly shooting curious glances at Jane.

"So tell me," Hazel asked Jane quietly, "what was this dishy lawyer's name?"

"What? Oh. It's really not important. It was such a long time ago." Hazel continued to look at her, gently enquiring. "Well – Oliver, since you ask. Oliver Grant. And I don't imagine he's dishy now. Probably fat and bald." She was irritated to hear a slight catch in her voice. After all this time! "But really, I wish I'd never mentioned him. He's probably married with a dozen children by now. I think I'll just go and help Tracy out in the kitchen."

On the Saturday afternoon, Jane had arrived at the hospital and followed the signs to St Anne's ward, clutching the flowers she'd just bought. A smiling nurse looked up as Jane approached the Nursing Station and directed her to Chris's mother's bed. "She will be pleased to see you," she said. "Two visitors, when she wasn't expecting anyone at all!"

True enough, as Jane walked over to the bed a man

"Oliver. Oh, I'm fine," she mumbled, aware that she was blushing, and wishing that she'd put some lipstick on. Chris's mother was looking from one to the other, slightly puzzled. Jane thrust the flowers at her and started to introduce herself, in case the old lady had forgotten who she was.

"Well, I'll be off," Oliver said, still gazing at Jane, and Jane could not think of a way of asking him to wait. After all this time, to wait a little longer.

"…a power-of-attorney document," the old lady was saying sorrowfully. "When you get to my age you have to be sensible about these things…"

Jane made the right noises, said yes and no in the right places and asked how things were going, but – she couldn't help it – her mind was elsewhere.

She forcibly pulled herself together and gave Chris's mother her undivided attention, but she had to admit to herself that it was a relief when visiting time was over, and she could leave the ward. She said the right things as she was effusively thanked for coming, but felt guilty nonetheless. She was looking forward to making herself a nice pot of tea and being able to turn over the events of the

For a moment neither spoke. "Jane," he said. "I didn't expect... how are you?"

was just putting on his jacket and gathering up some papers.

"…I'll make sure you get a copy early next week," he was saying, then turned round and saw Jane.

For a second neither of them spoke. "Jane," he said at last. "I didn't expect… how are you?"

afternoon in the privacy of her own home. *Events!* She mustn't exaggerate. It was a momentary meeting, for goodness' sake! Half a dozen words… Just a meeting. The first for over twenty years. But at least he hadn't forgotten her. And he was still good-looking, she reflected.

Continued overleaf…

Not fat or bald after all! But what must he have thought of her? She glanced down at her weekend trousers and sweater. It could have been worse, of course. At least she'd washed her hair… She glanced up to follow a Way Out sign, and there he was, again.

"I was wondering," Oliver said

top, or getting the last appointment at the hairdresser's. She found herself wondering when the bubble would burst, and how she would ever survive if it did. How could she ever have thought of breaking off her engagement to this wonderful man? How could she have been so stupid?

She began leaving work on time and rushing to the shops or the hairdresser

tentatively, whether I might possibly buy you a cup of tea? And perhaps some cake? Hospitals can be such dreary places…" She paused, and he hurried on, embarrassed. "But perhaps you're meeting someone." He had glanced at her ringless hand, and then, quite suddenly, he'd put his hands on her shoulders and leaned forward and kissed her cheek.

"Come and have tea with me," he said, his voice a little lower, a little more husky than she remembered it. "Please."

It must have taken five minutes, Jane reflected later, for them to establish that neither of them had ever married, and that they had a lot of catching up to do…

Tea turned into dinner, and was followed by more dinners, lunches, theatres, and quite a few intimate suppers in one or other of their flats. People at work commented on the change in Jane: she had more colour, they said, and looking in the mirror she saw that it was true: Her eyes sparkled and her hair shone. She, who had worked late more often than not for the past few years, found herself leaving the office on the dot of five and rushing to the shops before they closed, buying herself a new

All that had been two months ago. Jane had missed the last book group meeting, of course, as Oliver had taken her to Paris, so she hadn't had a chance to

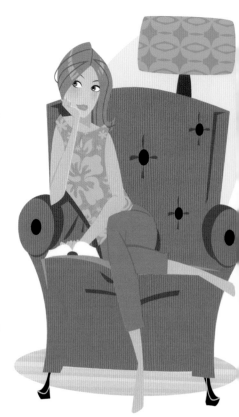

talk to the group about him. She made her way to Annette's house smiling to herself. She was just bursting to tell them.

She was the last to arrive, and the conversation stopped abruptly at the sight of her beaming face.

"You look like a girl with good news," Chris said expectantly. "Out with it!"

By way of an answer Jane waved her left hand at them, complete with its beautiful sapphire ring.

"That was quick work," Annette said, then added over her shoulder, "Haven't you got that bottle open yet?"

There was a loud pop, and Tracy was pouring champagne. All her friends looked delighted. But not surprised. Not even the tiniest little bit.

"Am I missing something?" Jane asked, looking suspicious. "You're acting as if you already knew…"

"Knew? Us?" Hazel asked with

going… You rotten lot, you set me up," she said, realisation dawning. "But you can't have known we were engaged," she said firmly. "We've been really discreet."

"She's a real gossip, that woman in the jeweller's, don't you think?"

Annette tutted. "People are entitled to their privacy."

"Honestly!" Jane said, shaking her head and smiling. "This is supposed to be a book group! It's more like a witches' coven! I've a good mind not to give you these," she added, handing out the wedding invitations.

"We've all learned a great deal about matchmaking from Jane Austen…"

pantomime surprise. "How could we?"

"You haven't even asked who I'm marrying!" Jane said crossly.

"You're right," someone else agreed. "Whoever could it be?"

"You didn't happen to bump into Oliver Grant by my mother's hospital bed, did you?" Chris asked innocently. "When he went to organise her power-of-attorney?" She paused. "He did seem rather surprised that I was so adamant that it should be him, and no one else from his firm. I gather he's a bit grand these days to do little things like that…"

Jane narrowed her eyes. "You rang me that morning to check what time I was

"Of course it's a book group," someone objected. "We've all learned a lot about matchmaking from Jane Austen. I think we've really got the hang of it now."

"Well," Jane said, almost lost for words. "All I can say… All I can say is…"

"Thank you very much?"

"Thank you very, very much."

A WORD FROM THE AUTHOR

"This story was based (loosely!) on my own book group, though I'm glad to say that so far we've left matchmaking well alone…"

The Way He Used To Be

Neither Ellie nor her mum was prepared for what they'd find at "grumpy Grandad's" sheltered housing…

By Sarah Swatridge

ou've conned me," accused Ellie, glaring at her mother.

"That's an awful thing to say," returned Carol. "He's your grandad and we haven't seen him for a while."

"But do we have to go *now*?" whined Ellie. "I only asked for a lift home from school. I didn't know we'd have to call in on Grumpy Grandpa."

Carol bit her tongue. She couldn't argue;

"Ten minutes will be fine," agreed Carol. "I'll just nip in and say hello and arrange to call back another time."

A few minutes later, they pulled up outside a brand new sheltered housing complex. "Wow!" said Carol. "This is so much better than his poky old house."

Ellie grunted but didn't look up.

"Are you coming?" she asked.

"No. You've got ten minutes." Ellie pulled out her phone to check her texts.

Carol counted to ten. She felt she needed the patience of a saint these days.

"All right, ten minutes. I'll just nip in and say hello and arrange to call back"

her father had turned into a grumpy old man. But he was still her father.

"We needn't be long," continued Carol. "I'd like to see his new place. It sounds wonderful." Ellie sighed a huge, teenage sigh. "And actually I'm feeling really guilty because we were on holiday when he moved and Auntie Sue helped him."

"Ten minutes, then," conceded Ellie.

It was Carol's turn to sigh. It wasn't as if Ellie was keen to go home to get on with homework, she felt sure – but with Ellie she had to pick her battles, and this wasn't one of them.

It wasn't easy having a teenage daughter, let alone a grumpy father as well.

Carol admired the pretty landscaped garden as she walked up to the entrance. It looked more like a five-star hotel than sheltered housing. She looked down the list of names on the buzzers and found number 7 with her father's name. Lawford Biddle. There could definitely only be one of those, she thought with a smile, as she pressed the button to be allowed in.

"You after Lawford?" asked a woman strolling in the garden.

"Yes, I'm his daughter."

"He won't be back yet," the woman informed her. "He doesn't get in until about four thirty."

"Oh." Carol was taken aback. "So where is he exactly?"

"Working."

"But he's retired."

"Oh, it's only voluntary work," she confided. "You know, at the hospital, but he's so keen he can't get enough of it."

Ellie couldn't get a signal. She'd opened the car door but that didn't make any difference, so she had to get out. There were some benches on the lawn. Ellie locked the car and plonked herself down on the nearest one. The other bench was occupied by two old dears, whom Ellie ignored until she heard one of them mention "Lawford".

"Put a bit of make-up on, perhaps

He welcomed her with a happy smile

Continued overleaf...

Lawford will notice you then," Mavis was suggesting to Dot.

"That's my grandpa you're talking about!" said Ellie out loud before she'd really thought what she was saying.

"Really? He's a lovely man," said Dot.

"A real charmer," agreed Mavis. "We've all fallen for him." She giggled.

"Ellie love, how nice of you to come and see me." His smile turned into a grin. "Come and see my posh apartment." He headed towards the glass entrance doors. "Afternoon, ladies," he said, touching his forehead as they passed Dot and Mavis.

"Afternoon, Lawford," they chimed and giggled again like naughty schoolgirls.

"I'm sure he'll always love your gran. But she'd not want him to be lonely"

"My grandpa's only got eyes for Gran," Ellie told them in no uncertain terms.

"I thought he was a widower," said Dot.

"He is. But he still loves Gran."

"I'm sure he does and always will," agreed Mavis. "But your gran wouldn't want him to be lonely, would she?"

"No," said Ellie thoughtfully after a pause. "I suppose she wouldn't."

She felt a tap on her shoulder. She spun round to find someone looking very like her grandfather. Except this man was smiling – and Grandpa never smiled.

"Dad!" Carol had been heading back down the path. "I see you've found Ellie."

"I'll give you The Grand Tour if you like," he said chirpily. Carol and Ellie exchanged looks. Obviously some alien had found its way into Grandpa's body.

"It's just a quick visit," began Carol. "Ellie's got homework to do."

"That's okay," said Ellie. "I'm cool."

You weren't kidding when you said The Grand Tour," teased Carol. "This is a wonderful place."

"You haven't seen my pad yet." He laughed. Yes, her father actually laughed.

So far he'd shown them the communal lounge and craft area, the gym complete with games console, the shop, hair salon and restaurant. When they'd got to the internet café he'd stopped to chat with some of his new friends – all female.

"There are only me and Ernie," he explained. "All the rest are ladies, so the ratio is about thirty to one." He chuckled.

"No wonder you sound a bit more perky," admitted Carol.

"It's not just that," her father told her. "Look at this place." Proudly he showed his daughter and granddaughter around his flat with en-suite wet room. "If I want a bath, there's a spa bath downstairs. It's got electric bubbles!" he told them.

"And I understand you've got a job," said Carol. Ellie looked surprised.

"That's thanks to Ernie," said Lawford

sixty-six so all the ladies are falling over themselves to be friends!" She paused. "Dad said he hasn't been so popular since he first got his army uniform and all the girls thought he looked so handsome."

"Tell me more about this job."

"Oh, I think you need to see that for yourself," replied her sister.

Carol was heading for the hospital help desk when she heard a "toot toot" behind her. There was her father, in what looked like a driver's uniform, driving a little train along the corridors to help those who were not so mobile.

"Fancy a ride?" he asked. "Isn't she a beauty?" He stroked the steering wheel.

"It's lovely," said Carol, smiling, inspecting the adapted milk float.

"It's very nippy on corners," he explained. "Ernie's got the new one but my customers don't have any complaints."

"Dad said he hasn't been so popular since he first got his army uniform"

mysteriously. "Come to the hospital between two and four and I'll show you."

Carol couldn't wait until the following afternoon to find out more about her father's job, so she rang her sister. "I can't get over the difference in Dad," she said.

"It's a lovely flat, isn't it?"

"The whole place is wonderful. It's more like a hotel than sheltered housing. I told Ellie I'm putting my name down!"

"He wasn't sure if he'd like it because he didn't know anyone and the lady in the housing department admitted there was only one other man there."

"Yes," said Carol. "He mentioned Ernie."

"Ernie is in his eighties and Dad's only

"Come on, Lawford," said one of his passengers. "I've got an appointment at the eye clinic at quarter past."

"Sorry, must dash." He gave Carol a salute and a wink and was off.

Carol smiled. Her dad had always wanted to be a train driver – and now, at last, his dream had come true.

A WORD FROM THE AUTHOR

"My Aunt Mollie retired to a great place. When she moved there, she was always out getting the 'old people' their pensions and beating everyone at Scrabble!"

ILLUSTRATIONS: ISTOCKPHOTO, MANDY DIXON

Standing In Sunshine

Have you ever wondered what might have been, if only you had made a different decision years ago? Rosalyn did…

By Louise Stevens

Slow down," Rosalyn said suddenly. "Turn left."

June crunched the gears of the hire car until it jerked to a halt, both offside wheels scraping the white kerbstones. She wound down the window fully, drawing in the intense afternoon heat.

"Well? Is this the place?"

"Yes," said Rosalyn, hesitantly. "But it's… different."

"It's bound to be," said June, checking her make-up in the rear-view mirror. "After thirty-five years. So where's this bar you wanted to see again? After that drive I need a long, cool drink."

"Straight ahead," Rosalyn answered, shielding her eyes from the sun. "The red building, with jasmine round the door."

"That? A dingy little fishermen's bar, you said," June replied, peering at a smart, open-fronted establishment, overlooking the beach.

While June smoothed her long, dark hair and re-applied bright red lipstick,

Rosalyn climbed slowly out of the car.

"June," she ventured.

"What is it?"

"I'm not sure I want to go in."

"Well I am!" June declared. "Now that we've driven all the way here in this heat."

"It would be cool inside," Rosalyn conceded. "It always was."

She crossed the narrow road. June followed slowly, high-heeled mules slipping on the shimmering cobbles.

Three men, middle-aged and wearing smart, casual clothes, were in earnest conversation at a table near the door. The remains of three meals lay in front of them. They looked up briefly as June and Rosalyn entered.

"What did you expect? It's bound to look different after thirty-five years"

"Where shall we sit?" June asked.

Rosalyn was already heading for a table in the far corner, nearest the bar. One of the men left the group, taking up a pad and pencil, and waited while Rosalyn and June settled into their seats.

"Buenos días, Señoras."

Rosalyn returned the greeting.

"You have wine or sangria, if you like,"

Continued overleaf…

It felt odd to wander these streets again

she told June. "I'll drive back."

As the man wrote their order, a woman, wearing a white apron over her striking red dress, came from the kitchen. He handed her the paper, then rejoined his friends. The woman looked from him to June and Rosalyn, shrugged her shoulders and sighed.

"Men!" she said dismissively. "Talk, talk. All day, they talk."

"I know how you feel," June quipped. "My friend and I are golf widows."

"So sorry," said the woman, not quite understanding. She served their drinks then pulled up a stool behind the bar and began reading a paperback.

Is it how you remember it?" asked June, looking around.

"More or less. I didn't spend a great deal of time in here."

Rosalyn surveyed the interior. The candles in wine bottles had been replaced with stylish lights and the rickety wicker tables and chairs with ones fashioned from wood and leather.

paper; I applied on impulse. Besides, I hated that typing pool! The family weren't bad people to work for. And yes, I had a few hours off most evenings."

"It must have been quiet here, before they developed the resort. Did you make any friends?"

"One," Rosalyn answered, looking out across the road to the beach opposite.

The old wooden bench had gone. She'd been sitting there one evening, desperately homesick after three weeks on the island, when a voice said, "Holà."

She'd turned quickly, too late to wipe away the tears. He was about twenty, a little older than she was.

"You are sick?" he'd asked with concern.

Shaking her head, she'd turned back to stare out at the sea. But he didn't go away. He offered his hand.

"I am Luis. I may sit here, please?"

The hand felt rough to her touch.

"If you want," she'd replied casually.

"I see you before. I work in bar, this one," he'd told her, pointing to a sad little building, covered with peeling paint and

She'd left Luis that sunny day, neither expecting, or wanting, to see him again

"Did you get much time off, when you were a nanny?" asked June.

"Au pair," Rosalyn corrected her. "Long hours for pocket money and keep. The young couple were here for a year – he was something to do with property – and they had two little boys."

"You shocked everyone, going abroad to work," reflected June. "You weren't the adventurous type."

Rosalyn smiled.

"No. I'd never been further than Bournemouth. There was this ad in the

a ragged tangle of jasmine.

"How did you know I'm English?" she'd asked, not really caring.

"The man you work for, he builds the new hotel. I work for him also. Day time, I build. Night time, the bar. In my home, there is little work, no money. Now, many people come here. I work hard so my life is better."

Another drink?" June asked, cutting into Rosalyn's reverie.

"What? Oh, sorry – yes, please,"

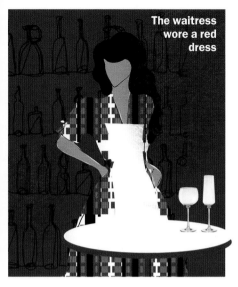

The waitress wore a red dress

"Did Graham know about this romance?" asked June.

"I told him, afterwards," Rosalyn replied.

Following that first meeting, Luis had seemed to be around most evenings, always asking permission to sit with her on the bench. Rosalyn began to look forward to seeing him. Eventually, he'd suggested she came to the bar.

In between serving the sparse customers, he would drink coffee with her and talk of his plans. He hoped one day to have enough money to buy a place of his own.

The local girls were rarely seen out alone and Rosalyn's presence earned some stares from the fishermen. But eventually, they'd turned back to their food and their conversation, which was usually accompanied by raised voices and a great deal of arm waving.

She'd asked Luis what they were arguing about.

"Anything." He'd laughed. "Politics, women, the price of fish."

It hadn't mattered that there were no cinemas or clubs, she and Luis just strolled barefoot along the warm sand, watching the twinkling lights of fishing boats, soft waves rolling in only yards away, all amid the heady scent of jasmine.

On one such night, just as it was getting dark and she was about to leave for the villa, Luis had drawn her to him and kissed her, and she'd wanted it never to end. But suddenly, he'd pulled away.

"What is it?" she'd asked.

Then he'd told her about Marissa – the girl he'd known for many years, from the same village. Luis's parents had already spoken to hers. It was expected that he and Marissa would marry one day.

Continued overleaf…

Rosalyn answered her distractedly.

"Are you reminiscing?"

"Sorry, June. I was just thinking about… someone."

"Really?" June whispered, leaning close. "Was it a holiday romance?"

"I wasn't on holiday. I was working. But, yes, it was a romance."

"Serious?"

Rosalyn nodded.

She'd left Luis that day to return to her employer's villa, neither expecting, nor wanting, to see him again. After all, there had been someone waiting for her back in England.

She'd started to see Graham while at school, although, as far she was concerned, it was nothing serious. Besides, Graham was studying most evenings, working at his apprenticeship.

But to her surprise, he wrote to her regularly. It might have been homesickness but, until she met Luis, Graham's letters had been the highlight of her week. He always finished his letters by saying he was missing her and looking forward to her return.

"Do you love her?" Rosalyn had asked.

"She is a nice girl," he'd explained. "I like her very much. This is our way, Rosalyn. Girls do not go out, meeting boys. When we see someone, the parents must approve and then it is agreed."

"But do you love her?" she'd repeated.

He stroked her face. "I did not mean this to happen, it will cause much talk, but… I love you, Rosalyn."

Afterwards, Rosalyn had lain in bed at the villa, imagining how it would be to live permanently on the island, with none of the things she took for granted back home – and lives, especially women's, governed by tradition. But her answer to every negative was: *those things wouldn't matter, if I were with Luis.*

Luis had taken her to meet his parents. They were scrupulously polite, but the anxiety on their faces was unmistakable.

"Give them time," Luis said.

But after just four months, her job had come to an end.

"My wife isn't coping," her employer explained. "The heat, no social life, no shops. She and the boys go home in two weeks' time. She'll take you with her, of course," he'd added.

When Rosalyn broke the news to Luis, he'd pleaded with her to marry him. Rosalyn had said "yes" and for a few glorious hours she'd truly intended to stay.

The next morning, though, she had tried writing to her parents, to tell them she planned to marry a man she'd known for three months and live on a foreign island where she had no other friends.

Reading back her own letter had forced her to admit the truth. It was all too quick, too uncertain.

Luis promised to wait, convinced that she would change her mind and return to him. And she so nearly had done, back in the cold, wet autumn of 1975.

But there was Graham, also waiting patiently, while the months turned into a year and Rosalyn readjusted to life back in England.

They became engaged. She was married in white. They had three children. It was a good, solid marriage. Only sometimes, in her secret soul, Rosalyn imagined she could hear rolling waves and feel soft sand beneath her feet and a young man's arms enfolding her.

A raucous argument at the other table jerked her back to the present.

"I wonder what that's all about," said June, nudging her.

"Politics, women, the price of fish – who knows?" Rosalyn replied. "I remember the men here getting very passionate. Arguing, I mean."

"Rosalyn!" June laughed at her. "You've made yourself blush."

There was a dull thud. The woman behind the bar stooped to pick up her book.

"I think she was asleep," June

The men always argued

whispered. "Another drink before we go?"

"Better not," Rosalyn answered, checking her watch. "Graham and your Sam said the tournament would finish around six, and we'll need to change for dinner."

June paid the bill. The proprietor nodded courteously as they left.

Outside, Rosalyn took a few steps in the direction of the beach.

"June," she asked, "do you ever

one-sided kiss told me it was pointless. "Wake me if you get lost," she said.

Back at the bar, the midday break was over, the men were returning to work. "Hasta mañana," they called as they left. The proprietor cleared the plates and walked back to the bar. In passing, he touched the woman's shoulder in a familiar, wordless caress. She smiled, brushed his hand with her cheek, and watched him disappear into the kitchen.

June leaned back in her seat. She too was remembering that summer of '75

wonder how your life might have been, if you'd made different choices?"

"Never," June replied. "I've learned to take life as it comes."

"I'm sure you're right," said Rosalyn, turning back towards the car.

They got in. June started fumbling with the air-conditioning while Rosalyn reversed and headed back towards the main highway.

"Can you find the way?" June asked, basking in the cool air.

"Relax," said Rosalyn.

June leaned back in her seat, eyes closed. She too was remembering that summer of seventy-five.

I'd always liked Graham, she thought. *I know it was wrong; Rosalyn was my best friend. But,* she reasoned, *she'd chosen to leave him behind.*

I'll never forget that midsummer party. Graham was looking so lonely, so I danced with him in the garden, smiling at everything he said, moving closer and closer, until it happened. Afterwards, I never dwelt on what might have been. That

Two glasses were left on the table. One had lipstick on it. She went over and picked up the other glass.

"Rosalyn," she whispered.

He used to murmur your name in his sleep. Do you think of him still? Is that why you came here today? You could not have made him happy, as I did. I was not too proud to take him back. Maybe you both loved, all those years ago, but it was a fleeting thing. You met again today, and did not recognise each other. So forget what might have been, Rosalyn, and enjoy all that is. Adios.

"Marissa," the man called. "Are you coming to help or not?"

"Yes, yes," she answered. "Have a little patience, Luis."

A WORD FROM THE AUTHOR

"I'm suggesting that the recollection of an old love affair is something to be treasured, but nevertheless is best where it belongs, in the past."

Her New Best Friend

There's something very odd about Emily, the uninvited guest… so why is she there?

By Camilla Kelly

"You're here!" I dropped my groceries onto the kitchen table and rushed forward to greet my sister. "I'm sorry I wasn't here to meet you, I got held up –"

"No problem," Zadie said, squeezing me hard. "I've still got a key." She gazed around the old family home. "I can't believe you're moving back here."

"I haven't the heart to sell it. And I love it – the garden, the woods, the privacy…"

Zadie rolled her eyes. She'd escaped to urban life as soon as she was old enough. Our mother, too, had recently emigrated.

"But the house needs so much work," she said doubtfully. "And…"

I moved to the window to see my little niece with another girl in the garden, making daisy chains. Fern was in the middle of telling a very energetic story.

"Who's she talking to?" I said, slightly annoyed. It was just like Zadie to bring an extra guest without any warning.

"Oh, that's Emily. Fern's new best friend." Zadie rolled her eyes. "They do everything together. *Everything*. It's driving me crazy."

"Emily," I repeated, hoping it was clear from my tone that I wasn't at all pleased about this ambush.

"I know, I know." Zadie held up her hands as if it weren't her fault at all. "But since the divorce, you know, I think it's good she has someone to talk to. And I

"She seems sweet. In fact, she'd be just about perfect if she wasn't imaginary"

"Oh, come on!" I laughed, knowing what she was going to say.

"No, I'm completely serious! My spooky sense, Rosie, I'm telling you…"

I'd heard about Zadie's sensitivity to ghosts ever since we were little, but I'd never actually seen any proof.

"I was hoping you'd help me redecorate while you're here," I said, smiling at the thought of Zadie getting her hands dirty. "Fern would enjoy painting, wouldn't she? Where is she, anyway? Outside?"

think Emily's okay – she's not leading Fern astray or anything."

Zadie helped herself to a peach from the bag of groceries and sat at the table to eat it.

I looked at the two girls. Fern seemed all elbows and skinny knees. The other girl was more childishly compact, her hair white-blonde.

"She seems sweet," Zadie went on. "In fact, she'd be just about perfect if she weren't imaginary."

I quirked a puzzled smile.

They were busy making daisy chains

"What do you mean, imaginary?"

Zadie laughed and wiped peach juice from her chin. "I mean not real, obviously. Do you see anyone with Fern?"

I looked at the girls, then back at Zadie. My scalp prickled.

"I don't understand."

Continued overleaf…

Continued from previous page

"It's quite common, apparently. I'm trying the technique of humouring Fern, acknowledging the IF."

"The what?"

"Imaginary Friend."

"Zadie, you're joking."

"I know, I feel ridiculous, but…" She shrugged, just as Fern came skipping into the kitchen.

"Hello, Auntie Rose!"

She threw her arms around my waist, pressing her cheek to my shoulder.

"Hi there."

The other girl, Emily, stopped in the doorway. We stared at each other.

"Can we go upstairs?" Fern asked Zadie eagerly.

"Sure. We'll call you for dinner."

Fern raced up the stairs, Emily behind her. I finally breathed out.

"She'll be building another one of her dens." Zadie patted my arm. "Thanks for humouring her."

The next day my neighbour, Dean, came over to help pull out some fitted cupboards in the bedroom. Zadie and Fern were going to help repaint the room afterwards, but right then Zadie was making phone calls downstairs and

"She didn't have anyone to look after her. I said we would," Fern informed me

I'd never understood Zadie's "spooky sense" before, but I felt it now. Emily, apart from her size, and shape, and face, didn't really look like a child at all.

She smiled serenely at me.

Fern released me and glanced at Emily. "Emily wants a hug too."

I stayed where I was. Goosebumps rose along my flesh.

Emily came and hugged me just the way Fern had. I let my arms hang at my sides, my body shrinking away from her. I didn't know what else to do. I stood there, feeling Emily's head – firm, but without any warmth – against my diaphragm.

"Do I get one?" Zadie said. She squeezed Fern until she squealed.

"Your turn, Emily," Zadie said, addressing a patch of air where Emily wasn't standing. She circled her arms as if embracing an invisible brown bear.

Emily stepped under Zadie's arms into the circle and gave Zadie a gentle hug. Zadie didn't feel anything.

Fern was outside with Emily.

I'd tried to talk to Fern last night while Zadie was out of the room. But Emily was always around. She'd even had a place set for her at dinner, and she certainly appeared to eat, although at the end of the meal her plate was just as full as it had been at the beginning.

"How did you make friends with Emily?" I'd asked Fern.

Fern shrugged. "She came home with me one day."

"You don't know where she came from?"

"She didn't have anyone to look after her. I told her we would."

Emily had smiled at me, as if to agree that she'd been lucky to meet Fern.

"And…what kind of things do you talk about together?"

Fern giggled. "Everything."

Now, I took Dean to the window and pointed down to the girls. They were playing at the edge of the woods, moving in and out of sight of the house. Fern was

collecting materials to build a den.

"So…that's Fern…" I said cautiously, hoping desperately that Dean would say, "And who's the other girl?" But he didn't.

"She's sweet," Dean remarked. "She looks like you."

I chewed my lip. Dean had become a close friend recently and if I was going to tell anyone my worries, it would be him. He was open-minded enough not to make me feel stupid.

"Listen, this might sound mad, but…do you see anyone with her?"

"No! No…" He saw I was upset and took my arm, gently guiding me to sit down on a paint can.

"If Fern can see her, why shouldn't you?" he said kindly.

"Because she's imaginary."

"Fern's dealing with her parents' divorce. Maybe she's feeling lonely. She needs a friend."

"I understand that."

"That's my point. You've moved recently, taken on a big responsibility. Maybe you can relate to her feelings – and that's why you can see Emily too."

I couldn't help smiling. He was making me feel calmer already.

I said, "But I've got you."

He slipped his fingers into mine and smiled. "Lucky you."

I rested my head against his shoulder. "But what do I do about it? I mean, what if Emily's something not so… friendly?"

"Maybe you should be nice to her. At least until you know for sure."

I wanted to talk about it more, but Zadie came to join us. She caught us sitting close together and gave me a meaningful look. I coloured and moved away from Dean.

"So what do I do about it? What if she's something that's not so… friendly?"

Dean took another look. "No. Why?"

"Fern has an imaginary friend called Emily. The thing is… I can see her, too."

Dean was quiet, processing this. I pointed down into the garden. "Look: right now she's showing Fern some sycamore seeds."

He said, very slowly, "I only see Fern."

"You think I'm crazy."

Between us we got a lot of work done, though Zadie complained about spending her holiday this way, and Fern was easily bored and kept insisting, "Emily wants to go outside."

Dean had to leave in the afternoon.

"I'll dump the cupboards outside," he said, gathering up the scrap wood.
Continued overleaf…

Continued from previous page

"That's so kind of you," Zadie said, with a flirtatious smile. Once Dean had gone, I smacked her on the arm.

"Hands off – he's mine."

"I knew it!" Zadie cried, laughing.

beginning to come undone. She was shaking, pale, chewing on her fingers.

I sat her down and gave her the phone.

"Call the police. I'm going to go deeper into the woods."

"She's hiding, made a den somewhere." Zadie's voice was high. "I'll kill her…"

For a couple of hours we continued painting and kept up the sisterly teasing that both of us denied we missed when we were apart. I even forgot to worry about Emily for a while.

Eventually it grew dark. Zadie pushed her hair off her forehead, leaving it smeared with paint. "I'll call Fern in."

"And Emily," I muttered.

For most of the afternoon I'd ignored Fern's friend, although occasionally I'd stepped politely out of her way.

"I know it's a pain," Zadie said. "But I'm sure Fern'll grow out of it soon." For the first time I saw the strain on Zadie's face. This wasn't easy for her.

I began to close paint tins while Zadie went to find Fern. A couple of minutes later she returned, puzzled and concerned.

"I can't find Fern. She must have gone into the woods."

We checked the garden again, and then the woods, calling out Fern's name. We came back and checked every room in the house, every cupboard and hiding place.

"She's made a den somewhere," Zadie said, her voice high. She laughed, as though to brush off her rising anxiety. "She's hiding, I know it. I'll kill her…"

One more search, top to bottom, inside out. By now Zadie was

I knew how horrible the thoughts going through Zadie's mind must be, but there was one fear I had that wouldn't occur to Zadie: What had Emily done to Fern?

I entered the woods, past the threshold Fern had been warned not to cross. I was barely into the trees before I caught a glimpse of movement in the dense bracken. I cautiously went towards it.

"Fern?"

I moved closer until I could see more clearly through the trees.

Not Fern, but Emily. Beckoning me closer, her face sombre.

Why wasn't Emily coming towards me? Was she trying to draw me in?

But then I had another thought. I'd never seen Emily without Fern. Maybe Emily couldn't be separated from her.

Right now Emily was shifting on the spot, agitated that I'd stopped.

"Come," Emily said. "She's here!"

The sound of her voice was jarring. She sounded so much like a normal girl.

I ran towards her, thinking only of Fern.

Emily went ahead, leading me to a withered tree that Zadie and I used to climb as teenagers. Emily stopped at the base of the trunk. Half hidden in the tall grass was a pile of old wood – pieces of the cupboards that Dean had taken down earlier.

I glanced at the branch above my head. It was freshly splintered and broken.

I looked at Emily. She pointed into the ditch behind me.

could have been worse. As it was, she could come home that same evening.

"Thank God you found her when you did," Zadie said, hugging me.

I didn't answer.

I waited until Zadie went to the pharmacy before I returned to Fern. For the first time since she'd arrived at the house, my niece was alone.

I sat next to her and took her hand. I had to say this, just once, because I'd never be able to tell anyone else.

"Emily helped me find you."

"I know she did."

"So…I guess she's a real friend."

Fern looked at me. To her, Emily had never been anything less, but her eyes were astute, as though she understood it wasn't that simple for me.

Perhaps Emily had only meant to be around long enough to help Fern. Useful though Emily had proved herself, I couldn't say I was sorry she'd gone. But I wondered if Fern would miss her.

I had to say this, just once, because I'd never be able to tell anyone else, ever

"Fern? Are you there?"

A faint voice answered. "Auntie Rose?"

I skidded a few feet into the ditch.

"Are you okay?"

"I was building a tree house…" I tried to follow her voice. "I fell…"

"It's okay, I'm coming."

I could see her now in the twilight, her crumpled little body in the ditch, half covered by bracken.

"I'm coming, Fern. I'm coming."

Fern was lucky. She had just a few scratches and bruises and was shaken by the fall, but the doctor said it

Right then Fern didn't seem too upset.

"I wonder where she's gone," I said.

Fern seemed puzzled. She glanced at the empty chair beside her. Then she ducked her head, hiding a smile.

She just shrugged and said, "She could be anywhere."

A WORD FROM THE AUTHOR

"The bond between childhood friends is always intriguing – especially if there's something a bit spooky about it…"

When We Meet Again

It's always been an emotional relationship, but has the heroine of this thoughtful tale reached the end of the road?

By Ali Anderson

T he storm has wrecked the garden. The paper bin has blown over and the hedge and trees are decorated with shards of soggy newspapers. I try to fix it, tidy things up, but the winds are gale force and nearly take me off my feet. Every time I stand the bin up it is bowled over again. My hands are stinging as I try to grab the lumps of sodden paper. Just as I capture them they're whipped away in another blast of icy wind.

know you don't like to be kept hanging around. I must try to keep tension to the minimum; avoid any messy conflicts.

The hot bath water is a welcome relief; I dunk my head right under and love the feeling of being completely clean. I lie back and listen to the silence of my empty house and all its little noises.

It's as though the house is breathing with me, having its own separate life that will go on when I leave today. Will it welcome you back, I wonder – or does it, like me, relish the silence?

When you went the first time I cried, hung round your neck, semi-hysterical

Another five minutes and I'll be running late, but I make one last endeavour to restore order out of chaos, unwilling to give in. Soon this solitude will be ended; you'll be here with me, in what was once our garden but what feels like my own space now.

I tear myself away and wonder just how I can possibly be late for something so important. The familiar stomach-churning starts and I wonder if I can fit in a ten-minute yoga meditation before I leave. Better get ready first, though. I

Then I become the woman I will be today, applying foundation, subtle slicks of tawny eyeshadow, a touch of pinky gloss on my lips and a hint of Dioressence to make me smell like a woman. My hair shines as I blast it dry in the tumbling mane you like so much. The lilac dress I bought last week looks fresh and springlike; I spruce up well.

I remember when you went the first time and I cried, hanging around your neck, semi-hysterical, hardly able to bear **Continued overleaf…**

to spend a night apart, as though I'd been bereaved. I was like half of a pair of scissors without you, somehow getting through the cold nights with my empty heart, struggling to see my way through the day without a text or a chat. I was smiling all over when you came home. *I'll never leave you again,* you promised, but we both knew it would come – probably sooner rather than later.

I'm ready now and the churning's started in earnest. By this time tomorrow

Do I have time for a quick meditation?

Continued overleaf…

it'll all be done and solitude will be my gift, if I want it. Just get through the next twenty-four hours and it'll all fall into place. My new life; squeaky-clean and ready to roll. It's what I've promised myself and so it will be.

table with a cup of tea and sometimes the book I'm reading. It's as though I'm in a bubble and nothing can touch me.

The churning resurfaces as I put my cup in the dishwasher and head for the back door. I want to stay in this moment,

You couldn't sleep. I'd wake to find you sitting in the kitchen staring into the dark

I have a few minutes before I have to leave; precious time to breathe. I walk the rooms of our perfect little house, tidying as I go, then finally settle in my favourite place at the kitchen table. The garden is messy again, I see, with all my carefully tidied papers swirling around and hanging from the trees.

I always feel so safe here, at my old oak

You started to change

safe and secure, without a thought for the future or the past. Doors locked and all the time in the world to potter. Maybe I've been left too long alone here, and it's made me peculiar. I hold my head up and breathe deeply as I open the door and stride out.

The ringroad's busy on the way to the airport. It'll be rush hour coming back, but you'll be driving. I'll be back to the passenger seat.

I've an hour of solid driving ahead. Every day is split into manageable blocks of time; my old trick to help me get through. This road is filled with landmarks from past years – the first, the hotel that I stayed in with Mum and Dad when we had weekend shopping trips to the city. There was always a show on the Saturday night and an Italian lunch the next day before we headed for home. Then there's the zoo, where we used to meet for cheese rolls and coffee, with an ice cream before we went back to work. I loved your uniform; my handsome soldier.

The second tour was where you changed. Little things, like being cross that I'd left the hall light on. And you couldn't sleep. I'd wake to find you in the kitchen with a cuppa. Sat at our lovely oak table, just staring out at the darkness. I tried to reach you to talk, but you were behind a brick wall, far away.

Then you threw the cup against the wall.

After that I was cagey, always wondering what would set you off, trying to keep things calm and pleasant. It had never been an effort before. I could only breathe again when you'd left, yet I'd yearned so long for you to come home.

A tree has blown over, blocking a whole lane, and my churning starts in earnest as things will start off badly if you're kept waiting. Yet I smile as I take the detour past the Happy Frog; we'd often lunch at the Chinese buffet when you came home from exercise. You'd joke that I could eat you under the table; you a

tetchiness, another spell of insomnia. This time it was whisky, not tea, and it didn't hit the wall, it was your fist that hit me. Just the once. But one time too many and one that I'll remember. Not the throbbing in my face. It's the pain in my heart that hasn't healed.

And so I draw up at the terminal to collect my husband, the war hero. Seven tours of duty in Helmand Province, a hundred bombs disposed of and a thousand or more lives saved. You look cheerful and I'm on time, so I can breathe easy.

You look at me in the way that always melted my heart, call me princess and take me in your big arms for a bear hug.

"Fancy the Happy Frog, skinny?" you ask, and I know that maybe I can do it one day – change my life – but not on this leave; after all your tours are finished. I

You give me the look that always melted my heart and take me in your big arms

big seventeen-stone man, me a slight eight-stone lady. It tickled you pink when I could beat you appetite-wise. The staff knew us there; Miss Little and Mr Large, they called us.

We haven't been in the past year. The Afghan tours take it out of you, you don't want to venture far or see anyone when you get home. Just me and you – that's how you like it.

You never forget the first blow, never erase the pain of being struck by the one you love. One blow, that's all it takes to kill the trust and tenderness. It happened in the kitchen. Another bout of post-tour

need to find out if the man I adored just fell by the wayside for a while, or if he never existed.

I suppose this is what you call love.

"Why not," I beam up at my handsome man. "We'll be just in time for dinner."

A WORD FROM THE AUTHOR

"No outsider can ever know what goes on inside a marriage, what makes it work or what holds those two people together – for better or for worse…"

ILLUSTRATIONS: THINKSTOCK, MANDY DIXON

It Takes Two To Tango

There's nothing like an activity-filled holiday with a bossy sister to help a lonely woman take a fresh look at life…

By Linda Lewis

By the time they reached their chalet, Susan was having second thoughts. She hadn't stayed at a holiday camp since she was a teenager.

"Remind me, what are we doing here?" she asked her sister.

"Helping you get over Mike," replied Rachel, who being two years older than Susan was used to taking charge. "Hurry up and get unpacked, then we can put our names down."

We'll soon find you a new man."

"Thanks, Rachel. You're the best sister a girl could wish for."

"Don't thank me," she replied. "My Jack's away with his mates playing golf. You're doing *me* a favour."

As they unpacked, Susan thought about her husband. When Mike said he was moving out, she'd been upset… but hardly surprised. Since their youngest child had left home, they had nothing left to say to each other.

They had spent almost every evening

"We're going to put our names down for everything. We're here to have fun!"

"What for?" asked Susan.

"Everything," replied Rachel with a grin.

Susan wasn't sure what to say, so she just laughed. "I thought we'd come on holiday to relax."

"No way. You can do that at home. We're here to have some fun, my girl. By the end of the week you'll have realised you don't need Mike to be happy.

watching the television in silence. It was no wonder Mike was feeling fed up. If she was honest, she was too.

He'd moved out five weeks ago. Since then they'd spoken every day on the phone, but no mention had been made of when he might want to come home. She was already starting to wonder if the trial separation might turn into something more permanent.

She followed her sister down to reception, where Rachel put their names **Continued overleaf…**

The instructor whirled her around the floor

Lively

Continued overleaf…

down for all kinds of activities.

"Darts, fine; bowls, maybe; but dancing?" queried Susan.

Rachel grinned. "I know. I've always had two left feet, but I've been longing to try the tango ever since that gorgeous Mark Ramprakash was on *Strictly Come Dancing*."

That night, the sisters had their first dance lesson.

The instructor was in his late fifties, but what he lacked in youth he more than made up for in enthusiasm and energy.

"Good evening, ladies and gents," he said. "We're going to start with the waltz."

"Do we really have to?" somebody piped up. "We were hoping to learn the tango."

"There'll be plenty of time for the tango once you've mastered the waltz." The instructor clapped his hands. "Right then, let's get started." He quickly organised

years fall away. She followed the instructor's lead and he swept her out into the middle of the dance floor.

"See," he shouted to the class. "This is how it's done."

They danced until she was breathless.

"Thank you," she said, when they finally stopped. "That was wonderful."

"Wow!" said Rachel. "I'd forgotten how good you were."

"Me too," Susan admitted.

That night, they'd signed up for the doubles darts tournament. After two rounds, to their surprise they were still in the competition.

"Goodness me!" said Rachel. "You're scoring enough for both of us."

"Just as well," laughed Susan. "Your last three darts missed the board completely."

She threw another dart

"I used to dance with my husband, but it must be at least twenty years ago…"

everyone into pairs. Given the lack of male participants, Susan wasn't surprised to find herself dancing with Rachel.

During the lesson, the instructor went from couple to couple demonstrating the various steps.

When he reached, Susan he smiled. "You've done this before, haven't you?"

"Yes, actually. I used to dance with my husband, but that must be at least twenty years ago."

He nodded. "Well, let's see what you can remember."

As they began to dance, Susan felt the

which landed in the treble, leaving her needing double sixteen to win.

She took a deep breath, aimed, and let the dart fly. When it landed bang on target, her sister cheered.

"I don't believe it," crowed Rachel. "We're in the final."

"I don't believe it either," admitted Susan. "I played darts with Mike when we first married. It must be twenty years since the last time we played. I'd forgotten how much fun it is."

Half an hour later, they were awarded first prize and a trophy to take home.

Susan hugged her sister. "Thanks so much for suggesting this holiday. This is exactly what I needed."

The next day they took an archery lesson. Susan had never tried it, and struggled to hit the target.

recognition. Now she spent two or three evenings a week doing all the things she used to do twenty years ago – taking part in quizzes, going dancing, playing darts.

As she stepped up to the oche, she glanced over at her partner. He smiled

As she stepped up to the oche, her partner smiled and blew her a kiss

Rachel grinned. "I'm glad you're not good at everything," she joked. "How are you at quizzes?"

Susan smiled. "Not sure. I haven't played for…"

Rachel finished the sentence for her. "At least twenty years. In which case, we're sure to win."

And that's exactly what happened. By the end of the week, they'd won prizes for all kinds of things.

As they were packing up to go home, Susan thanked Rachel for coming up with the idea of the holiday.

"I've had a great time."

"Good. I'm sorry we didn't find you a new man, but it has helped you get over Mike, hasn't it?"

"I'm not sure," replied Susan. "I'll have to let you know."

A month later, Susan was down at her local pub, playing darts.

"Beat that!" she said as another dart landed in the treble twenty.

Since going on that holiday with Rachel, her life had changed beyond all

and blew her a kiss. Her second dart hit the double, winning them the match.

Before she could react he was hugging her, right there, in front of everyone.

Her love life was finally back on track, and it was all thanks to that holiday.

The first thing she did when she arrived home was call Mike and suggest they start playing darts together again.

He said yes straight away. Now they were doing all the things they used to do, twenty years ago.

Rachel had been wrong. Susan didn't need a new man. She was more than happy to have the old one back again.

A WORD FROM THE AUTHOR

"On holiday, I saw a very elderly couple, waltzing round the dance floor. That made me wonder why I didn't dance any more…"

ILLUSTRATIONS: MANDY DIXON, THINKSTOCK

The Golden Rule

Boy meets girl, girl meets boy, boy likes girl, girl likes boy – what could possibly keep them apart?

By Jennifer Bohnet

From the day he walked into his office at Sage Machines plc, David Matthews made his position quite clear. He was not available for an office romance. Other people might find the idea of love by the photocopier a turn-on, but as far as he was concerned, it was a no-no.

To say Lisa Lewis was relieved by his attitude was an understatement. She'd lost count of the number of men who'd made her working life a misery in the past, with their innuendoes and their wandering hands placed oh-so-casually around her shoulders as they explained something or other to her.

an intimate moment. But David's businesslike manner never slipped. Theirs was a good working relationship, nothing more.

Within just six months of David's arrival, when they had made their department the most profitable in the company, their names were constantly being linked together professionally as they were held up as the ideal example for other departments to follow.

Looking at David now as she joined him for a meeting, Lisa wondered if he'd ever broken his "no romance in the office" rule. She had to admit that, under other circumstances, she might have made an effort to lead him astray… She shook herself and tried to concentrate

Even Lisa speculated about those deep chocolate-brown eyes focusing on her

But David Matthews was true to his word. The office was the place where he worked. The only relationship he wanted within its walls was a working one. Flirting with any of his co-workers was not on his agenda. He treated them all politely and kept his distance.

Of course this behaviour had the effect of making every woman in the building besotted with him.

Even Lisa found herself speculating how it would feel to have those deep chocolate brown eyes focused on her in

on what the MD was saying.

When the Human Resources department organised a weekend seminar, David was asked to give a talk on relationships in the workplace.

"I'm afraid it means a night away," David apologised to Lisa. "I hope you're not doing anything on the twelfth?"

Lisa shook her head. "I'm surprised I'm included. You're the expert on working relations. Do I really have to come?"

"Definitely. They'll want to hear how it works from your point of view."

So businesslike!

Lisa sighed. These events, in her experience, were viewed by most men as a chance to take advantage of any available women and generally behave badly while they were away from home.

David misread her sigh and looked concerned. "Will your boyfriend object to **Continued overleaf…**

you going away for the weekend?"

Lisa shook her head as she thought about Rufus, the man in her life – or he was on the rare occasions that she fitted into his busy schedule as a freelance computer consultant.

"Rufus isn't around to bother. It's just that overnight conferences with bosses and secretaries tend to be hotbeds of…"

David interrupted her crossly. "You know my views on office affairs, Miss Lewis. That won't alter because we're staying in a hotel together."

Lisa regarded him gratefully. "I wasn't actually thinking about you and me.

replaced his standard pinstripe, soft leather loafers his usual black shoes. Away from the office he was definitely another person.

She leaned back on her seat. Had David left his office manners at home, along with his normal working gear? Wickedly, a tiny part of her couldn't help hoping he had.

The hotel was an old country mansion, set in acres of rolling green countryside. Once they'd settled into their rooms, they made their way to the library to be ready for the first afternoon session of the conference.

As he spoke he flashed her an unexpected smile, bringing a flush to her cheeks

Other men aren't usually so thoughtful."

"Just tell me you'll come," David said gravely. " And I promise to act as your personal minder. You'll see – I won't allow any man, lecherous or otherwise, within fifty yards of you."

Lisa laughed. "All right. But one hint of sexual harassment and I'm off."

The hotel was a couple of hours' drive down the motorway and David elected himself chauffeur.

"I'll pick you up at ten o'clock. That should give us plenty of time to stop for lunch on the way too."

The open-top MG was a surprise. Lisa would never have associated him with such a sporty car. But it suited David to perfection in his off-duty persona she decided.

An expensive lightweight suit had

David, Lisa was amused to note, had changed back into his usual office attire. As he took his place on the stage, Lisa found a seat at the back of the room and settled down to watch proceedings.

Mainly she watched David. He was a very good public speaker. Once or twice he flashed her an unexpected smile, bringing a flush to her cheeks.

Later as they mingled with delegates David was true to his word, staying at her side protectively and defying any man to move in too close.

"This evening is free for people to do their own thing," David said. "I thought we'd have dinner here in the hotel if that's okay?"

"I don't mind dining alone," Lisa said. "If you want to join the other men in a night on the town…" But David shook his head.

"I wouldn't dream of abandoning you. Besides, I prefer your company. Eight o'clock? I'll wait for you by the bar. See you then." And he disappeared in the direction of the reception desk to make the table reservation.

When Lisa joined him in the bar for a pre-dinner drink David was once again wearing casual clothes.

"You look terrific," he said, eyeing her fitted red dress with its scooped neckline appreciatively.

"Thank you," Lisa said.

The maitre d' showed them to a table hidden away in an intimate alcove, out of sight of the rest of the dining room.

David, Lisa had the distinct feeling that she was on a date. A date that she was enjoying very much. It was with a start that she realised it was nearly eleven o'clock when David stood up, held out his hand and said, "Bedtime, I think. Come on, I'll see you to your room."

Outside her door, David gently touched her cheek.

"Goodnight, Lisa. I really enjoyed this evening. Sweet dreams." A kiss lightly brushed her lips, and he was gone – leaving a bemused Lisa staring after him.

It was the first time in six months he'd ever touched her. The first time, too, that he called her Lisa, and not Miss Lewis. As for that goodnight kiss – had he meant anything by it?

For the final question and answer session next morning, David asked Lisa to join him on stage. Together they answered questions on how they made their office relationship work so well.

There was just one sticky moment when David was asked by a particularly arrogant man, "Surely you must have been tempted to make a pass at Miss Lewis – she has obvious charms. Or are you gay?"

"Surely you must have been tempted to make a pass at charming Miss Lewis…"

"Thought we'd have some privacy in here," David said by way of explanation.

"And that?" Lisa asked with raised eyebrows, indicating the bottle of champagne nestling in its ice bucket.

"My treat – don't worry, it's not going on expenses! Now, what would you like to eat?" and he handed her the menu.

Sitting there eating and laughing with

Lisa gasped at the man's rudeness.

"No," David answered quietly, looking at Lisa. "And yes I have been tempted to make a pass at Miss Lewis, but, as I've said, office romances can cause more trouble than happiness. And I wasn't prepared to sacrifice an excellent working relationship for," David hesitated

Continued overleaf…

Continued from previous page

before continuing, "For something that could cause problems for someone I'm very fond of."

The chairman of the seminar leapt to his feet and hurriedly brought the session to an end, before saying, "David – could I have a word, please?"

Lisa collected her suitcase from her room before making her way downstairs to wait for David.

He was in the foyer talking to the chairman. As she approached she saw them shaking hands.

"Goodbye, sir. And thank you. I'll be in touch tomorrow."

Turning to Lisa he asked, "Do you mind if we have a quick coffee before we leave? There's something I need to talk to you about."

Businesslike as ever, David came

What next?

For a confident man he looked distinctly worried as he waited for her reply

straight to the point. "I've been offered a job in Human Resources at Head Office," he told her.

"Congratulations," Lisa managed to say, her thoughts in turmoil. So their perfect working relationship was about to be destroyed. "Promotion?"

"Right-hand man to the personnel director. It means more money, shorter hours. And…" David hesitated, glancing at Lisa anxiously. "As we wouldn't be working together, there'd be nothing to stop us seeing one another. Would there?"

For a confident man, he looked distinctly worried as he awaited her reply.

"You mean have an out-of-office affair?" Lisa asked wickedly.

"No I don't," retorted David angrily. "I

mean a serious relationship. Get to know each other properly."

Lisa nodded happily. "I'd like that. But it still gives me a problem."

David took her hand in his as he looked at her, puzzled. "What?"

"Where on earth am I going to find another secretary as efficient as you are, Mr Matthews?"

A WORD FROM THE AUTHOR

"Living in the countryside and working from home as a full-time writer, I don't miss office politics – but an IT department to fix my computer would be good!"

ILLUSTRATIONS: MANDY DIXON, THINKSTOCK

Teatime Treat

CHOCOLATE CARAMEL

GREAT FUN FOR KIDS!

Millionaire's Sandwiches

Ingredients

- 175g unsalted butter, softened
- 75g caster sugar
- 250g plain flour
- ½tsp salt
- 100g pack milk or plain chocolate chips
- 150g milk or plain chocolate, broken into chunks
- Small chocolate stars, to decorate
- 225g canned caramel filling

Preparation time: 30min
Cooking time: 12min
Makes 15

● Preheat oven to 180°C, Fan Oven 160°C, Gas Mark 4. In a bowl, beat together **butter** and **sugar** until well blended. Gradually work in the **flour**, **salt** and **chocolate chips** until the mixture forms a firm dough.

● Turn on to a floured surface, form a smooth round and roll out to 5mm thick. Cut out 30 rounds or stars.

● Arrange on a baking tray, prick with a fork and bake for about 12min until golden. Allow to cool on the baking tray.

● Put **chocolate** in a heatproof bowl and melt over a pan of simmering water. Remove from the saucepan and cool for 10min.

● Carefully half-dip each shortbread in melted chocolate and place on a board lined with baking parchment. Sprinkle with **chocolate stars** before the chocolate sets. Chill until fully set.

● When ready to serve, spread **caramel filling** over half the shortbreads and sandwich together with the remainder.

FOOD STYLING: KATHRYN HAWKINS PHOTOGRAPHY: LIGHTHOUSE

On This Day

On a dark and dangerous night, these two newlyweds are wondering if they will ever complete their journey to the inn

By Christine Sutton

he lashing rain was as sleek and shiny as jet and James rubbed his brow, beginning to find the wipers' monotonous thud dangerously hypnotic. In the seat beside him, Clare stirred.

"Are we nearly there yet?" She sounded like a small child minutes into a long journey and he smiled.

"Think so, darling," he murmured, trying to conceal his unease. "According to the map there's a turning on the left. Don't think I can have missed it."

The pretence seemed to convince her because she snuggled back under the rug. James peered into the darkness. It seemed they were heading straight for the edge of

snatched at the wheel, jamming his foot on the brake as they tore around the bend. The car slewed sideways and he fought to straighten it, grunting as he felt it respond. Just as he was congratulating himself on his driving skills, a bolt of lightning rent the sky, throwing the scene ahead into sharp relief. Ten yards ahead was a young lad.

For a moment James sat frozen, until Clare's scream jolted him into action. Yanking at the wheel he pulled sharply to the right. Divots of earth spattered the windscreen as the tyres gouged a path through the verge. For one terrifying moment it seemed they might turn over, then, astonishingly, the car was settling and they were heading on down the slope into blackness thick as pitch.

"Are you all right?" he rasped, not daring

Newly married, newly come of age and newly able to drive; it was too much...

the world, so impenetrable was the gloom. When two disembodied orbs appeared at the side of the road he jerked back in alarm, only to curse himself for a fool when the lights revealed nothing more sinister than the fluorescing eyes of a dazzled rabbit. How he regretted having accepted his brother's offer to borrow the motor. Newly married, newly come of age and newly able to drive; it was just too much...

"James, the turning!"

Clare's shout made him jump and he

to take his eyes off the road.

"Yes, darling. I don't know how, but I am. What's more, thanks to you, so is that boy."

"He is? You saw him?"

"Through the wing mirror. He looked petrified but he was okay, I'm sure."

"What on earth was he doing? He can't have been more than fourteen."

She shrugged. "Whatever it was, I doubt he'll hang around to answer questions. Let's just keep going."

Five minutes later they were pulling onto

the forecourt of the reassuringly solid, brick-built inn which was to be their home for the next five days. As the engine's purr died away, James slumped back in the seat and closed his eyes. It wasn't a journey he'd want to repeat any time soon.

Clare leant towards him, a hand on his thigh. "Well done, darling."

He dropped a kiss on her lips. "Come on, then, Mrs Baxter, let's go inside."

"Whatever you say, Mr Baxter," she answered, dimpling at the novelty of her new name.

The rain had eased and they darted through the puddles like skylarking children and ran lightly up the steps. Setting down the cases, James lifted the heavy metal door catch and pushed. The

Continued from previous page

studded oak door creaked under his weight but remained stubbornly shut.

"Perhaps they've given up on us and gone to bed," he said. "We are quite late."

"Let's both try," Clare suggested. "I don't fancy spending my honeymoon night on a doorstep." But just as they were about to

portraits with expressions more dour than the moth-eaten stag's head on the wall.

"Of course, Sir," Crowther chuckled. "Wouldn't be a country inn without a ghost or two, would it? Now, about that nightcap."

Crossing to the lounge, he threw open the double doors. In the room beyond,

James swerved sharply to avoid the boy in the road, almost crashing as he did

push again the door flew wide, dragging them over the threshold in a flurry of wet leaves. Turning to retrieve their cases, James heaved it shut.

They found themselves in a dark panelled foyer with worn, blue paisley carpet and four overstuffed leather chairs. Behind the counter stood a great bear of a man, with a cheerful, ruddy face, wild, sandy hair and eyes as bright as newly minted pennies. James estimated him to be in his mid-sixties.

"Welcome, Mr and Mrs Baxter, welcome. Come in, do, we've been expecting you. George Crowther, Sir, Manager and Licensee. Just sign there, if you would, and we'll see about getting you a drink. I'm sure you could both do with a wee dram to chase away the chills."

After the nightmare of their journey his warmth was as welcome as a mother's hug and James took up the proffered pen and scrawled his signature, adding an impulsive, *one half of the new Mr and Mrs Baxter!* for good measure.

"Spooky old place," he remarked, glancing over his shoulder. "Not haunted, is it?" All around were ancient

twenty or so people were silhouetted against a glowing log fire. Eager to enjoy its benefits James hurried into their midst, smiling and nodding as he went. Clare, though, hung back and, puzzled, he glanced round.

It was then that he became aware of how quiet it had become, as if the entire room were holding its breath. The stillness

126 *My Weekly*

intensified the smaller sounds; the shift of a log in the grate, the tiny click of the closing door. Then he heard Crowther say, "Ladies and Gentlemen, our guests are here."

His words were the signal for the pack to close in. Some reached out to almost touch, others circled them, their heads held on one side like inquisitive birds.

"James," cried Clare in alarm, as a thin stick of a man thrust his face close to hers.

"Shh," he soothed, slipping back between the shifting bodies, "it's all right."

Turning to face them, he began almost imperceptibly to retreat, hands held protectively behind him as he edged Clare towards the door. They were almost there, barely a foot away, when from the back of the room came a blinding flash.

All eyes swivelled towards the fleshy

aside, had first started to appear on the register. Time passed and registers came and went but with each anniversary there it was again, sowing in George the hope that this year, their fiftieth anniversary, James and Clare might finally complete their journey. That they had actually done so was beyond his wildest dreams.

The memory of that night was forever etched on his mind. A first-time poacher scuttling home to the hotel with still-warm eggs in his pocket, young George's shock at being caught in the car's headlights had nearly been enough to see him off there and then. He knew that, but for James's quick thinking, it would have been his ghost folk had gathered to see, and his sorrow was as much for the honeymooners' yet to be consummated love as for himself.

"James!" cried Clare in alarm, as they closed in, circling, trying to touch them

man clambering down from a chair.

"Blake, you fool!" bellowed Crowther, "I told you, no pictures. Now see what you've done." He gestured towards the empty spot where James and Clare had stood. "Photos are useless anyway," he stormed. "You know they won't show up on film."

"Worth a try, wasn't it?" muttered Blake, as the big man turned away in disgust.

"Worth a try?" Crowther exploded, rounding on him. "Worth throwing away five decades of waiting for?"

As the disgruntled party took up the cry, each condemning the snivelling Blake for his stupidity, George returned to reception to gaze at the signature that was all that remained of the Baxters' brief visit.

It was a year to the day after the fatal accident on Slippers Hill that James Baxter's name, together with its jokey

Sighing, he closed the book.

He was about to return to the lounge when something made him pause; the sound of laughter from the room above.

For a moment George stood puzzling. Then a smile creased his face. Taking a bottle of finest malt from beneath the counter, he poured himself a generous measure and raised it in a toast.

"Happy Anniversary, James and Clare," he said softly. "Enjoy your stay."

A WORD FROM THE AUTHOR

"Whether two weeks in the sun or a weekend in Blighty, every couple wants the perfect honeymoon. When things don't go as planned, love has to find a way..."

Well, Fancy That!

Does Emma *really* not want to go to the party… or does she just need persuading?

By Catherine Howard

The weather had been dry and sunny for days. It was far too warm to shut the windows. That meant Emma couldn't avoid hearing the music coming from a few doors down. The pulsing beat made her wish she hadn't turned down the invitation – but it was too late to change her mind. The party was fancy dress, and she didn't have a costume.

She wandered into the kitchen to make some coffee. Before the kettle boiled, the "I'll drop by on my way up, just in case you've had second thoughts."

Emma finished making her coffee and went back to her television programme. Unfortunately it was one of those complicated detective series where any one of half a dozen people could have committed the murder. She soon realised she didn't have a clue what was going on.

She turned off the TV and picked up her puzzle magazine, hoping that would keep her mind occupied.

When the doorbell rang, she expected it to be Susan. She was surprised to find

She braced herself for an argument. Her sister just sighed down the phone at her

phone rang. It was her sister, Susan.

"Have you changed your mind about going to the party? I'm just leaving."

"Even if I had, I couldn't go. I didn't hire a costume."

"So?" replied Susan. "I'm sure no one will mind. There are bound to be other people who haven't bothered."

"I know, but I wouldn't feel right. I've had more than enough time to get one," she said lamely. Lately even she could feel that her excuses were getting thinner.

She braced herself for an argument but Susan just sighed down the phone at her.

Matt Donaldson standing there, dressed as a cowboy, complete with Stetson. He worked in the same office as Emma's sister. They'd met six months ago at a wedding, where he'd done his best to try and chat her up. She'd turned him down flat. It was much too soon after her break-up with Daniel.

"Hi, Emma!" Matt said cheerily as he strode through the door. "Looks like I'm the first to arrive." He looked her up and down. "Have I got it wrong? I thought the party was fancy dress."

"It is. This is 21A. The party's at Dan

and Pauline's – they live at 12A."

"Ah." Matt looked very apologetic. "That explains why there's no music. Your sister gave me the address. I must have written it down wrong." He shrugged. "What must you be thinking of me, pushing my way in here like that? I'm lucky you didn't attack me with a poker."

Emma laughed out loud. Since when did anyone leave pokers lying about? Besides, Matt looked about as

threatening as a bowl of strawberry ice cream. And almost as attractive, she realised with a pang.

"Enjoy the party," she said, expecting him to leave, but instead he hesitated.

"Why don't you come too? I don't mind waiting while you get ready."

When she didn't reply, he covered his mouth with his hand. "Ah. Don't say I've put my foot in it again. You're not talking **Continued overleaf...**

Continued from previous page

to Dan and Pauline. Is that it?"

She smiled. "No. We're good friends."

She wasn't sure what to say. Her sister was right; she needed to start making more of an effort. After all, the party was only just down the road.

"I would go," she admitted at last, "but I haven't got a costume."

"So? We can always improvise. Let

emerged from her bedroom. "You look great. Turn round, and I'll fix your wings on." He attached the cardboard wings with safety pins, then helped her put on the crown. "There. Perfect," he said, handing her the wand.

Just then the doorbell rang again. This time it was Emma's sister, wearing a nurse's costume. "I see you changed your

Matt whistled appreciatively when she emerged. "I'll just fix your wings on"

me think for a moment." His forehead puckered into a frown. "We need cardboard and some kitchen foil." She led him into the kitchen and rummaged in a drawer. "Are these okay?"

He nodded. "Now, have you got a stick of some kind?"

"What for?"

"To make a wand. We're going to turn you into the cutest fairy princess the world has ever seen."

She giggled. It was like starring in an old episode of *Blue Peter*.

"There's a long wooden spoon, in the back of a cupboard. Will that do?" He nodded. "Sounds perfect. While you're there, fetch some scissors."

Matt cut out two wings from the card and covered them with silver foil while Emma made a crown. Bit by bit, the outfit took shape. The finishing touch was a large star which Matt stuck to the end of the spoon to make a wand. While he worked, Emma changed into a party frock and put on her make-up.

Matt whistled appreciatively when she

mind about the party." She grinned.

"Not really," Emma admitted. "Matt changed it for me. What do you think?"

"I love the wand," replied Susan with a raised eyebrow. "Very chic."

"Take no notice," said Matt loyally. "You look fab."

"Come on," urged Susan impatiently, "the music's calling me."

"Hang on," replied Emma, "while I fetch my keys and switch on the answering machine."

When they were alone, Matt turned to Susan. "I know what you did. I just wanted to say thanks."

"My pleasure," Susan replied.

She congratulated herself. All her sister had needed was a prod in the right direction. "Accidentally" giving Matt the wrong flat number had been one of her better ideas.

A WORD FROM THE AUTHOR

"When I was fifteen, I was invited to a fancy dress party and had to assemble a costume. That memory inspired this story."

ILLUSTRATIONS: ISTOCKPHOTO, MANDY DIXON

Fancy That!

Hallowe'en facts that make you go "**Wow!**"

■ **Anna Goddi was the last person to be executed in Europe for being a witch. She was hanged in Switzerland in 1782.**

■ In Mexico and Spain, Hallowe'en is known as Los Dias de los Muertos, or day of the dead, and is a day of rejoicing when people honour their ancestors.

Stephen Clarke holds the record for the world's fastest pumpkin carving time – an amazing 24.03 seconds!

The first person to bite an apple while bobbing for apples will be the first to marry

■ Dressing up originated from ancient Celts who dressed as demons and spirits to escape the notice of real spirits wandering the streets during Samhain.

■ **The equivalent to Hallowe'en celebrations in China is Yue Lan or the Festival of the Hungry Ghosts, during which food and gifts are offered to placate any ghosts who might be looking for revenge!**

■ **In the 17th century it was believed that witches used black cats as familiars to spy upon people and do their bidding, and many poor cats were burned because of this!**

Samhainophobia is a fear of Hallowe'en

■ **In Japan, the Obon Festival is dedicated to ancestral spirits, for whom special foods are prepared and lanterns are floated on rivers and seas.**

■ Folk born on Hallowe'en are said to enjoy second sight and protection against evil spirits.

Hallowe'en is a $7 billion industry in the USA, $2 billion of that from sales of candy!

Hallow means sacred and e'en is Scots for the evening before

Without You

Juliet made an agonising decision – to stay where she was needed, rather than start a new life. Was it the right one?

By Karen Byrom

November 19, 1962

Darling Peter,

Today, I went walking in the woods behind our old school… do you remember how we'd sneak out there on a Thursday or Friday, to escape double maths or a history lesson with "Droney" Jones? I haven't been there for ever so long, but this morning, after a week of dull, damp weather, the sky was bright and the air clear. I felt restless at home, and Mum didn't need me, for once… so off I went.

I'd forgotten how beautiful the woods are at this time of year, Peter. The leaves that still clung to the trees were all vibrant shades of red and gold, while those on the path crunched thickly and satisfyingly under my feet as I wandered along, kicking at them just like a child of five.

looking after Mum, I miss you every minute of every day. My darling, I wish you were here with me…

"Juliet." A frail voice floated across the hallway from the bedroom opposite.

With a sigh, Juliet put down her pen, picked up the paper she'd been writing on, and folded it gently in two. With quick, neat movements, she crossed to the dresser under her bedroom window, opened the top drawer, and laid the unfinished letter inside, with all the other letters she had written, but never sent.

"Coming, Mum." Carefully, she closed the drawer and went to see what her mother needed.

Despite the wheelchair and the hospital bed, and all the paraphernalia that accompanies an invalid lifestyle, her mother's room was bright and cheerful. Weak autumn sunlight filtered in through the pretty lace curtains to light up the pale

You've been gone nearly a year now, Peter, and every day has felt like a week

The experience quite gladdened my heart, until I remembered that you weren't there to share it with me.

You've been gone nearly a year now, Peter, and every day has felt like a week. In the woods, I've watched the ice melt from the streams, the bluebells bloom and fade, and the trees shed their leaves as winter approaches once more. No matter how busy I am at the hospital, or at home,

face propped on the pillows.

"I'm sorry to disturb you, Juliet," Nancy Carmichael said. "But I'm a little chilled. Could you close the window a bit, dear?"

"Of course, Mum," Juliet said cheerfully. "I'll fetch you a hot drink as well, shall I?" She suited her actions to her words and was soon sitting at her mother's bedside, sharing a warming pot of tea.

"It's a beautiful day for your day off.

She had forgotten how beautiful autumn was

What did you get up to this morning?" Nancy asked.

"A walk in the woods." Juliet laughed. "You should have seen the state of my shoes by the time I got home, all covered in mud and leaves. But it was glorious."

"The colours must be wonderful," Nancy agreed. "Did you go alone?" she added, with deceptive casualness.

Juliet, though, wasn't deceived.

"All alone!" she said cheerfully. "Peg's on day shift and Mandy's gone off to town with Dave." She pretended not to notice her mother's sigh. Nancy missed Peter almost as much as she did. For seven years, he'd been a constant presence around their home, ever since the day he and Juliet had started dating, back when they were just fifteen. But the older woman had stopped mentioning him. She didn't want to upset her daughter… just as Juliet herself refrained from saying his name in her mother's presence. She knew that Nancy still blamed herself for the rift, though she'd assured her mother time and again that she'd been just a small part of the decision she'd found herself having to make this time last year…

It had been a crisp autumn evening like this one that Peter had unexpectedly dropped by the hospital to walk her home after her day shift.

"Peter! I wasn't expecting you tonight!" she exclaimed happily.

"Got a surprise for you!" Eyes shining, he'd waved an official-looking letter at her. "I didn't think I'd hear for ages, but it came this morning…"

Continued overleaf…

"Oh, Peter! Have you got a job?"

Peter had been job hunting for months. Ever since the Beeching cuts that were affecting the whole country had closed down the railway line that served their small town, he'd struggled to find work, despite being a fully qualified engineer.

If he'd been offered a job, Juliet thought happily, then maybe they could start planning their future. She knew she wanted to spend the rest of her life with Peter, and was confident that he felt the same way, though he hadn't yet popped the question formally. She guessed he'd been waiting till he'd served his time – and then had come the news that his job was no more. Peter was proud; he wouldn't ask her to marry him without knowing he

Juliet – and think what a wonderful life it will be for us and our children!"

Aghast, Juliet snatched her hand away.

"Aren't you taking a bit much for granted, Peter?"

He looked puzzled.

"We are getting married, aren't we? We've spoken about it often enough."

"You've never actually asked me," Juliet pointed out. "But, Peter, I'm not playing games with you. I'd love to marry you, but I can't leave my mum and go to Australia. You know I can't."

Slowly, his grin faded.

"Juliet, I knew it would be hard for you. Your mum depends on you a lot, but there are plenty of other people. She could live with your brother or sister, or your aunt

Her eyes filled with tears. "I know it's been hard for you but I won't leave Mum"

could provide for her. It was difficult enough persuading him to go Dutch on their dates, even though she was earning good money as a nurse.

Now he caught her hand joyfully and pulled her into the small hospital cafeteria that served visitors and staff, refusing to say anything until they were settled at a table with a cup of tea. Then he brandished the envelope, grinning.

"It's more than a job! It's a new life – I've been accepted for Australia. I'm going to be a ten pound Pom!"

Juliet's own smile faltered as she took in the implication of his words.

"You're… you're going to Australia."

He took her hand. "Not just me. You, too! I'll go out there and find a job and a home, and then you can follow. They want nurses just as much as they want engineers. We can be married out there,

could come and stay with her. She lives on her own, doesn't she?

"I'm fond of your mum, Juliet, but we have our own lives to lead, our own future to look to… and there's no future for me here," he concluded a trifle bitterly.

Juliet shook her head slowly.

"I know how hard it's been for you, Peter." Her eyes filled with tears. "But I won't leave my mum. I've looked after her since Dad died, and it wouldn't be fair to make her move to Joseph or Michelle's home. She's talked about it before, but I know her heart's not really in it, no matter how much she pretends it would be a good thing. She'd feel too dependent."

"She's dependent on you."

Juliet shook her head. "It doesn't feel like that to me. I've never considered not looking after Mum – I suppose I always just thought that you'd move in with us both after we were married." She laughed shakily. "It seems both of us were making too many assumptions, doesn't it?"

They walked home in silence, each lost in their own thoughts – and regrets.

"I'll come round tomorrow night," Peter said squeezing her hand as he left her .

"That would be nice." She smiled sadly. "But I won't change my mind."

And she hadn't. She couldn't. Though Nancy herself more or less ordered her to go with Peter, declaring with false brightness that she'd be fine with her other daughter or son, Juliet kept to her decision. Her mum needed her.

Peter argued and pleaded, but wouldn't give in to her silent request to keep to the status quo. In Australia, he'd have prospects – and for a young man of twenty-two, that counted for so much.

"I'll write to you," he said sadly, the day before he left.

"No, don't." Juliet's voice was firm. "It's not going to work, Peter. Start afresh."

And with that blessing, she let him go. Then when she was alone, she cried until she could cry no more.

She couldn't resist writing, of course. Thoughts of Peter filled every moment, and she missed him more than words could say. But the letters were never sent. She went about her daily routine with resolute cheerfulness – only Nancy knew that her daughter's heart was breaking.

That was why, even after Peter had left for his new life, Nancy kept trying to persuade Juliet that she should follow him, that she herself would be well looked-after by the rest of her family and friends. But Juliet had laughed it off.

"I just don't want to live in Australia, Mum. I like my job and my life here. There's nowhere nicer than England."

"Even at this time of year?" Nancy's eyes twinkled. The winter had been long and hard, and Juliet was constantly bemoaning the long trudge in the snow to the hospital.

"Spring is nicer," her daughter concurred. "Daffodils and tulips and primrose… Or autumn. Think, Mum, if I went to Australia, how I'd miss the trees turn to red and gold." Was Nancy convinced? Juliet could only hope that she was. She never wanted her mother to feel a burden.

Anyway, she reflected wryly, it was true. The only attraction far-off Australia held for her was Peter. She was a homebird, through and through.

November 24, 1962
My darling Peter,

Early this morning, I went to the woods again. I wouldn't have believed it could be more beautiful, but a hard frost rimmed the leaves with an icy sparkle, and my breath turned to crystals in the cold air.

My hands might have been cold, but my heart was warm, Peter, and I could have climbed to the topmost tree branch for joy! I think you already know why.
Continued overleaf…

Continued from previous page

Your letter came this morning, Peter. I picked it up from the mat and examined its unfamiliar stamp. I didn't know what to do, at first. For weeks after you left I waited for a letter, despite all we'd said. Now you'd finally written it – and I didn't know what it would say.

Were you writing to plead with me to join you again? Worse, were you writing to tell me you'd met someone else? Your dad has never mentioned anyone, any time I've asked how you're doing, but still, it's been at the back of my mind.

I couldn't open the letter straight away. Mum needed her breakfast. But once she was settled, I took it up to my room.

Together we'll walk through the leaves

you missed me as much as I missed you. I can't wait to see you again... you said you were posting this letter from the ship, so you must be well on your way .

You say you're sorry for all the hurt you

Your letter came at last. I'm so glad you missed me as much as I missed you

My darling Peter, I can hardly write for tears – of happiness this time. I can't believe you're coming home, for me, when you've been doing so well out in Australia. But the new job you've been promised here sounds great. I knew there was a factory being built downtown, but I never dreamed you'd come back to work there.

How sly of Mum, to write to you about it! She never said a word to me until today, when I went bursting into her room to tell her the good news! Then she confessed she'd got Aunt May to get your address from your dad, and to post the letter she'd written to you. She reckoned that if she couldn't persuade me to go to Australia, then she should at least try to get you to come home. I've been so blind, Peter. My stubbornness hurt not only myself and you, but Mum, too. It's been hard for all of us.

But darling Peter, though it's been such a difficult year, I'm so happy to know that

caused me. Peter, I'm sorry, too, that I couldn't meet you halfway. But I'll be waiting for you on the quayside and together, we'll go walking in woods, kicking over the leaves as we kick over the traces of this last unhappy year. Together, we can plan our future at last.

Mum sends her love, and can't wait to see you again...

With a smile, Juliet folded the letter and added it to the others in the dresser drawer. It was a letter she could send, but she didn't have to.

Her beloved was coming home.

A WORD FROM THE AUTHOR

"Autumn is an ideal time for reflection, for saying goodbye to what-might-have-beens – and planning for a fresh beginning."

Teatime Treat

OLD FASHIONED DELIGHT!

Coffee Kisses

Preparation time: 25min
Cooking time: 15min
Makes 12 kisses

Ingredients
- 170g self-raising flour
- 85g butter, cut into pieces
- 85g golden caster sugar
- 1 medium egg, beaten
- 1tbsp coffee essence (or 1tsp instant coffee mixed with 1tbsp of boiling water)

Coffee butter cream:
- 55g butter, softened
- 115g icing sugar, sifted
- 2-3tsp coffee essence (or 1tsp instant coffee mixed with 3tsp boiling water)

FAMILY FAVOURITE

- Preheat the oven to 180°C, Fan Oven 160°C, Gas Mark 4. Line two baking sheets with baking parchment.
- Sift the flour into a large mixing bowl. Rub the butter into the flour until it resembles breadcrumbs and stir in the sugar. Stir in the egg and coffee essence.
- Make into balls about 2cm in diameter. Place on the baking sheet. Place in the oven for 15min. Remove to a wire rack to cool down.

- Make the coffee butter cream by putting the softened butter into a bowl and beating well with a wooden spoon. Stir in the icing sugar and mix well. Add coffee essence to taste.
- When the biscuits are cold sandwich two together with a little of the butter cream.

TIP! These treats can easily be transformed into lighter than air chocolate kisses – by replacing the coffee with a dessert spoonful of cocoa

RECIPE: FIONA BURRELL PHOTOGRAPHY: LIGHTHOUSE

Top Of The Bill

Is the lure of bright lights and leading roles too hard to resist, even for an ageing actor?

By Brenda Crickmar

 e's been a regular for about five years now but still somehow, even on this boring, heat-laden afternoon, he manages to light up the room as soon as he enters it.

Of course, I've always known he'd never be interested in me.

He's an actor. You might have heard of him: his name is Leslie De'ath. If you ask me it's the name that always held him back. Had his name been Will Hamilton

long and the colour of Guinness; the grey in it, showing up silver against the rest, only an enhancement. His nose is strong and bony and his mouth long and thin, with a certain cruelty about it making it interesting, rather than a threat.

The bar I work in the West End, is in the seedier end of theatreland, which is why Leslie De'ath is so often seen propping it up.

"Wow, it's hot! Oh, hi, Susie," he says now and gives me his special smile. A smile that says, *you're the only person in this bar as far as I'm concerned. You are*

Leslie gives me his special smile, the one that says you're the only person in this bar

or Daniel O'Neil, he'd be up there with the greats. He has the looks, the presence and the charisma. Boy, oh boy, he has that in spades. But the name Leslie just doesn't do it for anyone anymore, does it? You don't give Leslie Howard a thought; instead a picture of "great uncle Leslie" comes to mind. An elderly man with thinning hair and braces, a roll up in his mouth; old – even in the times of the Teddy Boys. Someone whose photo you might see in a fifties copy of *Picture Post*.

But the real Leslie De'ath is tall with blazing eyes. His hair is thick, a shade too

the most fascinating, most dazzling woman I have ever met in my life. Then he notices Camilla sitting in the shadows and flashes the same smile at her. She scowls back. She is a leading lady and only interested in producers or directors or actors in the top league. Leslie De'ath is no longer in the top league – if ever he was.

Leslie turns back to me. Meanwhile, I've poured him his usual vodka and tonic; I add plenty of ice. With none of his usual flamboyance he puts a note on the bar and tells me to have one myself. This time I think, maybe I will. This time

Leslie studies his drink, unsure how it got there

there is something different about Leslie De'ath, something subdued and a little disturbing.

It's very hot today; a sudden hazy heat reminding us that summer is still with us despite the recent rain.

Somewhat warily, I watch Leslie as he leans his threadbare corduroy cuffs against the dark wood of the bar. Why he chooses to wear the corduroy suit in this heat is a mystery. It's old, yet ageless, much the same as the lines on his face; a face that could pass for anything between thirty and fifty, and often has. He studies the drink in front of him as though unsure quite how it got there, as though he's forgotten having ordered it. Then he gives a shuddering sigh that starts down in his well worn boots and vibrates slowly through his body until it escapes his nostrils in a raw despair.

Continued overleaf…

"Oh Susie, Susie," he says giving me that look again, the one that says I'm the only person who can possibly understand him, the only one to whom he can unburden his soul. And he's right – at the moment I am. Apart from Camilla the bar is empty.

"Always the bridesmaid – never the bride," he says theatrically.

I wait for him to go on. I know he isn't speaking about me. It's he who is the important one here.

"Thought I had it in the bag. Beast of a part. Made for me. College lecturer of the old school."

Ah, that explains the suit.

"My agent said no one else stood a chance. Well, no fool like an old fool… It's gone to some prat from a soap on the box! Can you believe it?" He goes on bitterly. "All my years of experience don't count for a thing. If you're up against some brainless pretty face off the telly – you're scuppered – well and truly."

Leslie knocks his drink back in one hit and indicates that he'd like another. This time no money changes hands.

like you… We could maybe run a little riverside pub together. What do you think?"

Despite the sudden change in the tempo of my heart, I take care that my expression doesn't alter, and he looks away with a self-deprecating smile. "No, I suppose I'd drink the profits…" He stares dolefully into the distance, then excitedly he looks back at me again. "A B&B then? A seaside B&B."

For a fleeting second our glances meet. I move my glass on the counter to make a circle. Could it be?

We hold each other's gaze and my heart is beating wildly now.

Would it really be possible?

His elegant hand moves closer to mine and he starts to stroke my wrist with his artistically long fingers. I feel myself drowning in the hypnotic depths of his eyes.

"Why not?" he says eagerly.

Why not? There is surely nothing to stop me. My days in the chorus line have long since finished.

"What do you say? It'd be fun. A seaside town with a pier and a promenade. I could learn to be a Punch and Judy

"I can see it now; a small seaside threatre, our lives full of old-fashioned nostalgia"

Another sigh escapes him and he looks at me with eyes that are no longer blazing and put me in mind of my mother's spaniel. Leslie's eyes are wonderful, usually full of charm and good humour, but now as they search mine for reassurance, I can see that they're brimming with despair.

I make a sound half way between a sympathetic murmur and a cough.

"Oh Susie, Susie!" He leans a little closer on the bar and gives a long sigh. "I wonder if it's time I gave this life up… I could be happy you know, with someone

man. You could serve cream teas…"

For a moment I imagine a long curving promenade. I see the tide lapping on a sandy beach and hear seagulls screaming overhead. I can picture the horizon shimmering, and white sailed boats bobbing on the waves. The air around me smells fresh and clean, not sticky and sultry with heavy heat.

"Yes," he goes on warming to his theme. "I can see it now; a small seaside theatre. Maybe there'd be the occasional cameo role I could play. Our lives would

about casting you anyway."

My wrist might have been red hot because Leslie's fingers have ceased stroking it and his eyes no longer hold mine.

"That's terrif," he says and turns so that all I can see is his corduroy back. "That's great news." Apologetically he indicates the shabby suit. "I can glam up you know, if a cooler image is required."

The producer shows his teeth in an insincere smile. "Couple of things to discuss," he says. "Mineral water, please," he says to a point left of my shoulder.

I comply, of course I do; that's my job. It's what I get paid for.

The dream seaside image fades into the distance.

be full of old-fashioned nostalgia. We could grow old together amongst our theatrical memorabilia."

By now he's holding my hand in a strong grasp with one hand whilst still stroking my wrist with the other. The effect is potent.

I feel my lips curving into a smile indicating that I'm ready to allow myself to think about the possibility of such a mad idea. After all, we've known each other years. We have a history – of sorts – and we've always been friends.

The door to the bar bursts open. Sudden light pours in bringing a stale wave of London street heat with it.

"Holy…" says Leslie.

In the background I notice Camilla snapping to attention, her frown completely vanished.

"Thought I'd find you here," says the West End producer I recognise at a glance. "Charlie can't fit it in after all… I've been having second thoughts

And I watch as a pathetically grateful Leslie De'ath ushers the producer over to a corner table to discuss the play.

For another hour they sit in a huddle discussing the motivation, mood and perception behind Leslie's character. Then eventually I hear their chairs scrape as they rise to their feet and without a glance in my direction the producer leads the way to the door and opens it.

But Leslie looks back and smiles at me. "Come to the first night Susie? I'm counting on it."

"Of course," I say. "I wouldn't miss it for the world."

A WORD FROM THE AUTHOR

"The name Leslie De'ath fascinated me. It immediately conjured up a picture. An actor past his best, a lonely barmaid. Bingo – I had a story!"

The Perfect Gift

What do you buy for special parents who have everything?
Sometimes the answer is staring you in the face…

By Teresa Ashby

Laura's eyes twinkled with inspiration. "I know the perfect present for Mum and Dad. A fancy coffee machine."

"Oh, no," Claire shook her head. "Dad's not keen on coffee. You know how he prefers his cup of tea."

Laura's heart sank. Everything she'd suggested so far, her sister had instantly disagreed with.

"I know," Laura's husband said. "How about as it's their silver wedding anniversary we…"

"Be quiet, Tony," Laura said. "We're thinking. Why don't you go and make us a cup of tea?"

"Not for me," Claire said, rubbing her

"And I don't want to sound penny pinching," Claire added, "but we haven't exactly got a huge budget."

Claire was right. There were lots of things they would like to get for their parents if money were no object.

"I think it would be nice if…" Tony began as he brought in their drinks.

"Not now, Tony," Laura said.

Bless him, she knew he was just trying to be helpful, but she really needed to be able to think without him interrupting her all the time. And being a man it stood to reason he wasn't going to come up with anything sensible.

When the subject of the anniversary gift was first raised some months ago, he'd suggested a new washing machine as their old one made such a racket when it was spinning.

There were lots of things they'd like to get for their parents if money was no object

stomach. "It's a bit warm for tea. A glass of lemon juice would be nice though."

"We've got to think of something," Laura said. "How about a cruise?"

"Mum gets seasick." Claire chewed her lip. "Remember when we went on that boat trip when we were kids? She said she'd be happy if she never set foot on a boat again for the rest of her life."

"True," Laura sighed. "She gets a bit queasy if she has her bath too full."

But Laura and Claire wanted something extra special for their parents.

"Why don't you pop round and see Paul?" Claire said. "He's tinkering with his car and I'm sure he'd…"

Tony was out of the door and gone before Claire had finished her sentence.

"Wow, what did I say?" Claire said.

"The magic words." Laura laughed. "It's wonderful how well they get on, isn't it?"

"It is," Claire smiled. "They'll be

messing about with that car for hours now, so we should be able to do some serious thinking. What's that you're drinking?"

"Carrot juice."

"Carrot juice?" Claire cried. "But you hate carrots."

"I know," Laura said. "But they were doing a taste test in the supermarket last week and I tried some and now I can't get enough of it."

"Hey, I know," Claire cried. "How about a posh barbecue and one of those swing seats…"

Laura couldn't honestly think of anything worse.

"They're not really outdoorsy are they?" she said. "Dad's got a phobia about barbecues and you know how mum is about creepy crawlies. Besides, it's getting colder now so they wouldn't get much use out of it until next year."

"True."

"Perhaps we should get something silver," Laura said.

"Mum hates polishing and silver would **Continued overleaf…**

have to be polished. How about an annual pass to those gardens she likes visiting?"

"Dad gets bored going round gardens," Laura said. "And he reckons flowers make him sneeze. Maybe we should be thinking of something they can keep."

"Matching eternity rings," Claire said.

"Dad?" Laura laughed. "Wearing jewellery? His watch and his wedding ring are his limit."

Claire laughed and nodded. But they both stopped laughing and starting thinking. It wasn't funny really. They'd been talking about this for months and getting nowhere.

"We've got to think of something soon," Claire said gloomily. "It's their anniversary in a couple of weeks."

They'd spent hours looking at catalogues, more hours traipsing round the shops and yet more hours on the

"Well?" Tony asked. "Have you thought about what to give your parents for their wedding anniversary yet?"

"No," they choroused.

"Tony and I have been discussing this," Paul said. "A meal out might be just the thing for them."

"But that isn't something they can keep," Laura protested. "Besides, we were going to take them out for a meal whatever happens."

Their husbands were even more useless at all this than they were. Laura wished they'd just leave it to her and Claire. She was sure they'd think of something eventually. It was just a matter of waiting for that light bulb moment.

Tony grinned. "I hoped they'd have cottoned on by now, Paul. Honestly, and

"Haven't you cottoned on yet? Honestly, and they say men don't notice things"

internet trawling for ideas and still they remained uninspired.

"What about a vase?"

"But Mum's got loads of vases," Claire said with a sigh.

"Well I don't know," Laura said. "Our parents are impossible."

The door opened and Tony was back with Paul in tow still wearing his oily overalls. They were both grinning. Laura looked up in surprise. She thought they'd be busy all afternoon.

they say men don't notice things."

Laura felt a nervous little twinge. What was Tony on about? Surely he wasn't going to give away their secret just yet. They'd agreed to wait for a couple more weeks at least.

"Tony," she said warningly.

"Do you think you're the only one?" he said and turned to look at Claire who was sipping her lemon juice and looking a little sheepish.

"I have no idea what they're talking about," Claire said with a shrug.

Tony and Paul burst out laughing.

Paul sat down beside Claire and Tony perched on the arm of Laura's chair and put his arm around her.

"We'll book a table at the best restaurant in town," Tony said. "And we'll order champagne, but you won't be able to drink any so we'll get you some chilled carrot juice."

"Tony," Laura bashed him with her elbow. "Shut up!"

"Claire won't be able to have any champagne either," Paul said, his grin getting bigger by the minute.

Laura stared across at her sister.

"Claire – you're not…?"

"Yes I am," Claire said. "I was going to tell Mum and Dad before I told anyone else, even you Laura, and now Paul's spoilt my surprise and… why can't you drink champagne?"

Laura burst out laughing.

"For the same reason as you," she said. "And I was waiting to tell Mum and Dad before I told you. But I thought I'd wait until we'd got the wedding anniversary celebrations out of the way."

They hugged each other.

"Congratulations," Laura said, tears of joy rolling down her face. "I'm so pleased for you."

"And I am for you," Claire said happily.

"Well as I was saying," Tony said. "I think it would be nice if…"

"They're not listening," Paul said. "But I think it would be a wonderful present. One they could keep forever and…"

The girls broke apart. Laura looked at Tony. He and Paul were looking very pleased with themselves.

"You've had an idea?" Laura said. "Something Mum and Dad can keep? Something sensible?"

"Yes," Tony said with a grin. "A meal out with champagne, fine food and…"

"And?" Claire said.

"The news that they are about to become grandparents for the first time – not once, but twice over," Paul finished.

Laura and Claire were holding hands, staring at their husbands in amazement.

Laura had to admit that it had crossed her mind but it would have only been a special gift from her and she couldn't have left her sister out of it. But now she wouldn't have to.

"I think it's a wonderful idea," Laura said, squeezing her sister's hand.

"And how about a new washing machine as well," Tony suggested.

"Well they'll certainly need one," Claire said, laughing.

So it was decided.

Laura and Claire had always been close. They were only born eighteen months apart, but Laura had always felt very much the big sister and now her baby sister was expecting a baby of her own.

Laura was almost as thrilled about that as she was about her own baby and she realised she'd been so preoccupied with her own pregnancy and worrying about the wedding anniversary that she'd failed to see what was staring her right in the face.

Luckily for them though, Tony and Paul were more perceptive. They'd come up with the perfect gift – it had been there all along.

A WORD FROM THE AUTHOR

"Of course, I expected my mum to be pleased when I told her on Christmas Day that I was expecting her first grandchild, but she was so much more than pleased. It is one of my all time happiest memories."

Hot Stuff!

With hormones and hot flushes to deal with – and an errant husband – tonight was going to be a nightmare, wasn't it?

By Alison Henderson

argh! Why did it have to be tonight, of all nights, Hollie's glam party? Why now, when I'm old and done in, abandoned and ravaged by time? Jerry always said I was a drama queen and I guess he had a point.

I wonder if Blondie, the petite personal trainer that's my replacement, is prone to throwing wobblers. I doubt it. She's glam, smiley and gets everything she wants. There's nothing to strop about for her, really. She even got my mid-life crisis husband when she was supposed to be working on his waist line.

I feel another one coming on now. Relax and try to go with it, I instruct myself as a huge, horrible whoosh of

biceps and Minx nails (tacky, I reckon, with all that design on them. I've gone for French manicure tonight, on hands and toes). Reckon I've just got to grin and bear it – four and a half hours of my life, and tomorrow's another day – a bit like giving birth, really.

Sometimes I wonder if the whooshes made me crazy and drove Jerry away, but the Dirty Girls Crochet Club, my close inner sanctum of girlie pals – some abandoned, others fleeing for a little menopausal "me" time – all assure me that it was her, the wild weight trainer, that lured him from my comfortable grasp. Our Friday night meetings involve crochet and looking at hot men in chick flicks – there's nothing like "in, over, through and out" if you're having a crisis.

I don't look bad for an old bird, actually, despite ranting that I'm over the hill

warmth engulfs me and makes me feel all wrong. At this rate I'll look all sweaty and horrid when I get there. Blondie will be perfect and glowy while my make-up runs off in rivers. Oooh, life's a bitch!

I smile when I think of my Hollie, though. Twenty-five, just graduated and just engaged. With the big party tonight to celebrate it all how can I, as her mother, say I can't face it? Can't walk in to see my husband of twenty-five years with Little Miss Glam with her perfect

It was as he was going that these dreaded hot surges came on with a vengeance. My imbalanced hormones are deranged in a way that even a large gin and tonic will no longer soothe, so I'm scarily angry, alternating with hysterically weepy and suddenly sleepy. I'm just going to have to accept that that's the mad old bird that I am and make it through the evening anyway.

I don't look bad for an old bird, actually, despite ranting that I'm over the

hill. I've not succumbed to a thickening waistline or any of that stuff. Taking over the gardening and dog walking completely have left me leaner and slightly tanned. I'm not as young as Blondie but, soaring temperature or not, I'm going to give her a run for her money tonight. She'll never know I can hardly bear it. I try to latch on to this positive surge and rein in my rage to make it work for me. Well, it's better than crying, isn't it?

Continued overleaf…

I've opted for a red shift tonight. My blonde hair's been expertly French rolled and Elnetted so it'll take a real powerful flush to shift it in any way.

My make-up's pretty indestructible as well – waterproof mascara, Doublewear Perfect Foundation (if Mrs Lauder guarantees it won't move, then I believe her), my favourite Arden coral lipstick, all finished off with a spray of Oscar De la Renta. Oh, it takes me back. The husband bought it for me on our honeymoon and it's been my signature scent ever since.

Wonder what that little trollop wears? CK or something trendy that's been out five minutes, I reckon. Wouldn't know a

where we've had all our family functions but tonight there'll be an extra non-family member on the scene. At least she'll be on my territory, so I'll be kind and gracious for my daughter's sake.

Hollie looks so lovely – blonde curls pulled back from her face and cascading over her shoulders – perfect with her simple champagne dress. She's like a Greek goddess, my gorgeous girl. The solitaire on her finger sparkles and I remember when Jerry produced the little box over the dinner table and slipped my own diamond on that special finger.

"That's my heart," he'd said, and I never thought he'd ever leave me. Well, I'm ringless tonight apart from Granny J's

Avoid alcohol, all the hormone books tell you, but I'm going to sink a gin

classic if it hit her square in the face.

My Jerry always liked me in red. I've finished it off with a simple gold necklace and Granny Johnstone's pearl earrings.

The last evening we had together, I was wearing something similar. He'd been telling me all night I was looking lovely, before he dropped the bombshell that he hadn't been on the golf club trip to Portugal but had just got in from Ayia Napa where he'd been doing a workout with little missy.

That golf club has a lot to answer for; I knew he never took the clubs to the airport. Stavros the mini cab man was left in charge of every man's clubs while they hit the light fantastic. Any excuse for a drink without the wives. Stavros and I had a sly joke about it on many an occasion and I never really minded. Hubby took it too far when he went on a separate trip with Blondie though.

Tonight's a golf club "do" as well. It's

ruby on the other hand. Have to say, it's a cracker, and I've cleaned up well.

I'm arriving with Hollie tonight. Fiancé Mike will accompany his own parents, and the Dirty Girls Crochet Club are all coming as singles to support me.

Avoid alcohol, all the hormone books tell you, but I know I'm going to sink just one large gin when I get there, just for the nervous system, you understand.

Just do a last minute bag check to ascertain that I've got the tissues and the Clinique double compressed powder in case of any mega whooshes. If stress brings them on, then I'm on a losing battle, but I'll aim to stay cool!

Well, it's pretty weird but as the night goes on, I'm feeling curiously detached from Jerry and Little Miss Blondie. The Dirty Girls are in full swing, planning new throws to start crocheting next weekend and giggling at the thought

of a whole series of Jack Nicholson movies to leer at (forgive us, we're old and he's more our thing than Justin Bieber).

"What's wrong with a man with a bit of a tummy?" hoots Yvonne, recently left by husband number three, Andy, who went

He looks a little the worse for wear and strangely lost. They're playing *When I Fall In Love*, Granny J's favourite song and mine too.

"Dance, Marthie?" he asks and his eyes look nervy and desperate, darting around.

"What's wrong with a man with a bit of a tummy?" my friend Yvonne hoots

off to train husky dogs in Alaska and never returned.

"Nothing, I hope," my husband says as he materialises at our table, trendy shirt straining slightly, wiping beads of perspiration from his forehead.

"Yes," I smile graciously as he takes my hand and leads me to the floor.

Blondie's standing by the bar armed with a gold clutch bag and playing with a bling-type phone. I hadn't realised how **Continued overleaf…**

Continued from previous page

small she is before; skinny and short to the point of looking as if she needs proof of age to get in here.

She's trying not to look as I put my arms around Jerry's neck, the way I have one hundred times before. And a miracle has occurred as I'm not flushing. No big hot whooshes; it's Jerry who's sweaty and out of control and clinging to me like a lifebelt on the Titanic.

I look around and realise that I'm comfortable here tonight, at the party that's caused me sleepless nights for months, where I confront my husband and his lover,

while they jet off to party overseas.

"Ah, Marthie!" The cheery Greek applauds me and drags me back to the floor to whirl me around to Robbie Williams.

Jerry and Blondie seem to be having some sort of fandango at the bar but I don't really want to be nosy; he can be a bit of a handful with a drink, my husband.

Stavros is a widower and lives with his big Greek mama in Clapham. "You hot stuff, Marthie," he laughs infectiously and the dirty girls overhear and shriek – "Ooh, she is, Stav! Especially recently – really hot stuff!" I'm flushing with fun as Robbie belts out *She's The One*.

It looks like Jerry and Little Miss

I glance round and glow in the presence of my daughter, my family and my girlies

happy in their sparkling shiny life together.

For the last six months I've cried and cursed my crazy hormones, and raged over the man that left me for Blondie. But now she's hopping around ten yards away, casting frenetic glances at my big, pathetic hubby who looks as if he's drowning.

I glimpse Granny J's ruby sparkling on my index finger and glow in the presence of my daughter, my family and my girlies.

I disentangle myself from Jerry who seems to be having trouble letting go and head back to our table where Stavros who runs the mini cab firm is holding court with the girlies, telling outrageous stories about all the errant hubbies who have left him in charge of their clubs

Weights are leaving. She's running along behind him and seems quite distraught.

Stav keeps dancing and I do agree with the girlies that there's nothing wrong with a man with a bit of a tummy as I look him up and down and smile.

He's having such a good time and I'm sooo looking forward to The Dirty Girls Crochet Club next week – there's going to be too much to talk about!

A WORD FROM THE AUTHOR
"There's absolutely nothing like the force of our long-term female friendships! I think The Dirty Girls Crochet Club sounds like such fun, I'd love to meet them for cocktails!"

Fancy That!

Winter facts that make you go "Wow!"

The big chill

Icicles form most often on the south side of buildings

- A single snowstorm can drop 40 million tons of snow, carrying the energy equivalent to 120 atom bombs.
- According to legend, we will have a cold winter if birds are seen migrating early or huddling on the ground.
- Ten inches of snow melts down to one inch of water.

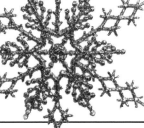

The tallest snowman was 113ft 7in tall. He was named Angus and was made in Maine in 1999

- Hailstones are built like an onion – the layers count the number of times it travelled to the top of the storm before falling to the ground.

Antarctica set the record for the world's coldest temperature at -90°C

- The record for the most snow angels at one time was set in Ontario, Canada, in 2004 when a couple of schools joined to create 15,851 snow angels.
- The wind chill factor measures heat loss from exposed skin.
- If it gets cold enough, single digits or below, ice crystals can form and snow can fall from clear skies.
- All snowflakes have six sides.

- Snowflakes fall at an average 3.1mph.
- Hot water freezes faster than cold water.
- Ice is a mineral.
- 60% of the Earth's fresh water is stored in the polar ice caps.
- The "winter blues" were first diagnosed in 1984 and have recently been ironically named seasonal affective disorder or SAD.

The world's biggest snowflake fell on January 28, 1887, in Ft Keogh, Montana. It was 15 inches across and 8 inches thick

Fairy Dust

Don't believe in fairy godmothers? Think again, because they can come in the most unexpected of guises…

By Lexie George

The girls exclaimed in unison when they first saw Alice, "What on earth is that?"

"She's my Christmas fairy," I replied, a little piqued.

"Mum," they explained pityingly, "Fairies have pretty sparkly dresses, not a toadstool skirt and a khaki tunic top. And where's her curly golden hair? All fairies have golden curls."

Alice, you see, had very short, dark and straight hair.

"Just look at her wings," I said defensively. "Of course she's a fairy."

hearty woman we'd bought the house from had boomed, "My dear, keep her on, good cleaners are like gold dust."

It wasn't just the cleaning though. Alice knew everyone in the village and reported such interesting snippets that I sometimes found it hard to tear myself away to go to my rather boring job. And she loved our cantankerous cat, Felix!

Then an evil stepmother cast her spell. My husband fell in love and left with a girl ten years younger than me who was also glamorous, rich and successful.

My eldest daughter reacted by shaving off her hair and dying the stubble deepest black. Her sister became quiet and

As I unpack the Christmas decorations, I fondly remember the year I made Alice

"Well, that's not a wand she's holding."

"No, it's a feather duster. Really it should have been a vacuum but my Blue Peter skills aren't that good. Anyway it looks a bit like a wand."

Shaking their heads at their sad mother, the girls disappeared upstairs, giggling together.

Now, as I unpack the Christmas decorations, I remember the year I made Alice. Up until that time I'd been lucky. I'd had a loving husband, great children and a beautiful house.

Also, of course, the real Alice. I'd never before had a lady who "did" but the

withdrawn. All of us lost a lot of weight. The country went into recession.

It took about a year to sort things out and divide the goods. He got his sports car, whacking great salary and pension prospects – and, of course, Her. I had the girls and the mortgaged house, my battered old estate, the cat and my part-time job. He did contribute to our expenses but I soon realised that my previously rosy financial position was drastically altered.

Alice and I sat sadly in the kitchen drinking tea whilst I told her I couldn't **Continued overleaf…**

My home-
made fairy
was truly
unique

Continued from previous page

afford to keep her on any more.

"I'll really miss you," I wept. I cried a lot in those days.

"I'll really miss Felix," Alice sniffed.

He and I watched sadly as Alice disappeared forever down the drive.

My ex-husband told me this was a

She still comes to visit – and help

A recession is hardly the best time to start up in business, but I had to try. I'd hoped to put the house on the market, downsize and pay off the mortgage, but nothing was selling.

"Think positive, go and talk to the bank manager," my ex advised, while I quietly gritted my teeth.

"I'm really sorry," the bank manager explained, "but I'm afraid that as a single mother with only a part-time job, you're just not a good credit risk. I have to consider my shareholders and there is a recession, you know."

So I started to think laterally and for myself. If the house wasn't selling I'd use it to start my own business, although I couldn't give up the day job yet. So "Cooking4You" subtitled "Freezer filling to banquet" was born.

Did I have any experience? Well, I loved to cook but I had no business skills, otherwise I'd have known that freezer filling meant I was mostly making 2 portions of 20 different items. However, I didn't feel much like sleeping

A recession is hardly the right time to start up a new business, but I had to try

good opportunity. I'd always, he reminded me, wittered on about starting my own business, so why didn't I do it now? I didn't like the implications of "wittered". Surely as an ex-husband he'd forfeited the right to make such remarks! I'd show him, then.

so I could easily fulfil the moderate orders I was getting. And the girls and their friends always had a variety of meals in the freezer.

That was September. October remained quiet, although I was asked about catering for a couple of office parties in December. This should have alerted me to the fact that Christmas was coming – and fast. By November my phone never stopped ringing.

I had such requests as, "Could you do just a couple of large-ish lasagnes?" or "I know it's short notice but I'm sure you can do me canapés for forty" and "My mother-in-law's coming to stay, help!"

It went on and on, which at first seemed great, but I soon realised that small orders take a lot of time but don't earn you much. I was desperate to clean

I cooked for as long as I could and then reluctantly left saucepans and dishes to soak, because I didn't have time to wash them before I left. I hated coming back to mess but I had just enough time to dash to the shops before starting work.

I'd never thought of a supermarket entrance as magical, but that was where I bumped into Alice.

"Are you all right?" she asked. "You look completely exhausted."

Willing my eyes not to fill up I replied, "Oh, you know what it's like at this time

Christmas was coming – and fast – by November my phone never stopped

the house and the ironing pile was in danger of falling over, but even managing on four hours' sleep I didn't seem to have any spare moments.

"We'll help," the girls promised, as they disappeared to their friends' homes. I reassured myself that if I could keep going until Christmas, life would slow down again after that.

But the second week in December my boss asked casually, "You don't mind doing an extra half day do you? Just until the Christmas rush is over."

I couldn't afford to lose my job yet so I meekly agreed.

Consequently on the Monday, when I had planned to cook all day, I only had the morning. I set my alarm an hour earlier, telling myself I could manage on a couple of hours' sleep for a few nights.

The girls called out as they left, "Don't bother about food for this evening, Mum, we're going to Donna's party."

Why couldn't I go to a party, too? It would take more than a fairy godmother and a pumpkin to get me to a ball.

of year, everyone's busy."

"Not me," she replied. "I'm going to my sister's this year, so I've no preparations to do at home."

Lucky you, I was thinking when she broke in with, "You couldn't do with some help, could you – just until Christmas?"

I stared at her speechless, financial considerations buzzing in my head. Then I replied as calmly as possible, "I don't suppose you've got time today?"

As she nodded, I realised I really believed in fairy godmothers, no matter how unlikely they might look.

She took my keys and flew away whilst I hurried to work.

I held my breath when I went in that evening. After all, how much could Alice have done in a few hours?

I realised just how much as I gazed around slowly. The ironing pile had disappeared. Everything had been put away. All the rooms were blissfully clean and tidy – and in the sparkling kitchen **Continued overleaf…**

Continued from previous page

she had even left the teapot and a mug out ready for me on my return.

"I am going to afford Alice again," I told Felix determinedly, and he agreed it was a brilliant idea.

"Please can you come for a half-day every week again?" I asked Alice when I took her money to her the next day.

"I'd like that ever so much," she said. "I've really missed your cat you know."

Just after Christmas I was asked to cook for a directors' dining room every day. This made all the difference, Cooking4You was now viable and I was able to give up my boring day job.

That Christmas hadn't been particularly good for me. I only had time to make my Alice tree fairy because I was on my own a lot over the

Better than a magic wand?

I think the tree wouldn't be the same without Fairy Alice – and the cat agrees

celebrations. There were no balls, so no Prince Charming appeared to sweep me off my feet. Life didn't change overnight, but it did start to change – albeit slowly.

All that was a long time ago and the real Alice still comes to visit – and help – occasionally. We laughed today as I took out her namesake to put on the tree.

The girls will be arriving soon and will no doubt protest again, but their children love Fairy Alice. I think the tree wouldn't be the same without her – and Felix's successor seems to agree.

"It's time you gave me a new hairstyle though, I haven't had short, dark hair for years," Alice said. "And my duster could do with a few more feathers."

Perhaps I will.

The girls now run Cooking4You and the directors' dining room, so I have lots more time. In fact I only cook for Richard, one of the directors who was so keen on my lunches he asked me to marry him!

So yes, I do believe in magic and definitely in fairies – but I also think my feather duster is more effective than any magic wand could ever be.

A WORD FROM THE AUTHOR

"We've downsized now and don't need a cleaning lady. The one I had did sometimes seem like a Fairy Godmother and she inspired me to write this story."

Teatime Treat

LITTLE TOPPERS

Little Christmas Snowmen

Cooking time: 15min
Makes 9-12

Ingredients
- 1 small pack fondant icing
- Red icing and milk chocolate, to decorate
- 300g white marshmallows
- 70g butter
- 275g crispy rice cereal
- 200g white chocolate
- Cake decorations

GREAT FOR THE CHILDREN

● On a flat surface, roll out **fondant icing** and using a pastry cutter, cut out a 2cm wide circle for each snowman. Draw faces on each, using **milk chocolate** and **red icing**. Set aside for later.

● In a large pan, stir the **marshmallows** and **butter** over a medium low heat until the mixture melts. Slowly stir in the **crispy rice**.

● At the same time, rest a heatproof bowl over a pan with simmering water. Add the **white chocolate** to the bowl and stir until melted and even.

● Take about 2tbsp of the mixture at a time and form into balls, then halve each ball to make a flat based semi-sphere for the body of each snowman.

● Dip the base of each snowman into the melted white chocolate. Set aside on greaseproof paper. Use small blobs of fondant icing to glue **decorations** to each snowman.

TIP! **To save time, use ready-made fondant icing, cake icing tube in red and packs of seasonal cake decorations to add detail to your snowmen.**

Switch On The Magic

When fairy lights start to twinkle, a little bit of love will just grow and grow and a whole world of possibilities can appear

By Stella Whitelaw

That man across the road is at it again. Look at his house! All those lights. Talk about environmentally-unfriendly. He takes the biscuit."

I peered out through a crack in the curtains. Being a nosey-parker neighbour is not my normal routine. I haven't even spoken to the man across the road and Kelly, Daisy and I have lived in this house for over a year.

Don't call me unfriendly. Call me busy. So busy, all I can manage at the end of the day is to make a cup of coffee and collapse in front of the telly.

environmentally-friendly way this Christmas." Kelly nearly tripped over the long word. Her reading is good, but a six-syllable word is quite a mouthful.

"So who is going to decorate our house in this friendly, non-electric way?" I asked, grating Parmesan. Daisy was looking very bored by the whole conversation.

"You and me, Mum. I'm sure we'll have masses of ideas," said Kelly, already mentally decorating the front of our house with loops of draped loo-roll.

"And you think I have time for this?"

Kelly snuggled up to me in her award-winning way. "You and me together. We're a great team. Your shop gets all its books delivered in bubble wrap, doesn't it? Yards

Kelly snuggled up to me in her award-winning way. "We're a great team"

"Have you seen the council competition, Mum?" asked Kelly, my eleven-year-old daughter. "We could go in for it. I've got lots of ideas."

"What competition?" I was making pasta with cheese and mushrooms for supper. Enough for two. Daisy doesn't eat pasta. She's ultra-fussy.

"The council are sponsoring a contest for the house decorated in the best

and yards of the stuff. We could paint it silver or white."

"Or white and silver."

"Drape it along windowsills."

"Icicles in streamers from the letterbox and from all the shrubs in the garden."

"Cotton wool for snow?"

"No, cotton wool is a fire hazard. How about that popcorn stuff they use for packing? Crumble it up to look like snow."

The shop gets masses of that. It's all thrown away."

Kelly gave me a hug. "I knew you'd have brilliant ideas."

"So what's the prize?"

"I've no idea. It's mercenary to be more interested in the prize than in the taking part." Thus spoke a philosophising eleven-year-old. "Is supper ready? Shall I lay the table?"

Daisy looked up with interest, alerted by the sound of cutlery. She loved cutlery.

The house across the road was in full swing with its Christmas decorations. Fairy lights strung everywhere, along the guttering, the roof, in the trees, winking on and off in the windows. It was enough to bring on a migraine.

The young man who owned the house **Continued overleaf…**

was out every evening, adding to the display of energy-wasting light. A portly Father Christmas appeared on the front lawn, going Yo-ho-ho in a growly voice every ten seconds.

"I like the Father Christmas," said Kelly. "Could we have a Father Christmas?"

The kitchen floor was a mass of popcorn snow. We were rolling handfuls in flour-and-water paste and shaping snowballs out of the stuff. Each one a handmade original snowball. Perhaps we could sell them as works of art? The Tate goes for weird ideas.

"I'm painting the wheelbarrow white and filling it with these snowballs," I explained. "That beats a Yo-ho-hoing

Christmas. He'd been so good at it, whereas I found the whole thing such an effort. And he'd been Christmas shopping when the accident happened. I couldn't bear to think about it. Some drunken driver going home from an office party.

"Okay, no bird frighteners. How about bird parties then, with lumps of fat hanging from the silver string?"

Even Daisy took an interest in these decorations and sat hopefully under the trees, evidently planning to give the birds a warm welcome.

The man across the road was building a sleigh on his roof. Kelly watched in increasing trepidation.

"He's going to fall off, Mum. Shall I go

"He's going to fall off the roof, fixing that sleigh. Shall I go and warn him?"

Father Christmas any day, hands down."

"It doesn't really," said Kelly, picking bits of industrial packing popcorn out of Daisy's mouth. She'd try anything for the taste factor. "But I could hide under the wheelbarrow and sing *I'm Dreaming of a White Christmas.* I know all the words."

"You are not hiding under any wheelbarrow. Now where are those bits of string from the shop? We're painting them silver to hang from the trees."

"What are they supposed to be?"

This stumped me. It had seemed like a good idea at the time. "I know. Milk bottle tops. We'll hang milk bottle tops from the string and sell them as bird frighteners."

"That's not a very nice attitude, frightening off the birds. Goodwill to all mankind – and birds, especially robins. Where's your Christmas spirit, Mum?"

My Christmas spirit was at a drastically low ebb. I missed Michael the most at

and warn him? It looks very dangerous. No sleigh on a roof is worth a broken leg."

"Or a broken neck," I agreed.

M y intrepid daughter trudged across the road and I watched her speaking to the man. He was not as young as I had first thought, seeing the flecks of grey in his dark hair – or was it artificial snow? He was nodding thoughtfully, and Kelly was pointing to his pond. He had iced over the pond with something white and luminous.

"He's going to have a skating sleigh," she said triumphantly on her return. "I suggested it. He thought it was a brilliant idea. Asked me if I'd got any more ideas."

"You can't change sides in mid-competition," I said. "Did you tell him he's wasting electricity? Electricity that poorer countries would be so happy to have."

"I did tell him, but he said something

about how do we get it to them?"

"Build power stations for them. Harness the wind, waterfalls, waves."

"I don't think Mr Mac is too good at that sort of thing. His sleigh is falling to pieces."

"Mr Mac?"

"He said to call him Mac."

"You'll do no such thing. Now get on with your homework. School doesn't come to a complete halt because Christmas is on its way."

My energy level seemed to have perked up quite a bit since entering this competition. We filled in a form and left it at the council offices – we still didn't know what the prize was. We planted white candles all over the garden with orange peel flames. We had to eat a lot of oranges, as they soon shrivelled up.

Nightlights in jam jars were another idea. We were fully stocked in case of any power failures in the future.

Kelly sacrificed her silver fairy fancy dress outfit which she had hung on to nostalgically for years. We cut it up to make shooting stars, with the bigger stars made from silver foil. The house was beginning to look like something from a magic book.

I say, your house looks terrific." Mr Mac was standing at our front gate, an admiring look on his face. "Inspiring, inventive, magical."

"All our own work," I said, stiffly. I would not be friendly to someone who didn't care how much electricity he **Continued overleaf…**

Continued from previous page

wasted. Funnily enough, his house wasn't bright with lights that evening. It was in pitch darkness.

I've come over to ask a favour," he said. "Could I please have one of your candles? I've fused everything. I can't even make a cup of coffee."

It would have been very un-Christmassy not to ask him in for a cup of coffee and a mince pie. Kelly was delighted to see him. She was making icicles to hang from the guttering and after coffee, Mr Mac got

I sent Mac home with a flask of coffee, a packet of candles and some mince pies.

The Mayoress, Mrs Irene Paxton, judged the competition, and Kelly and I were absolutely thrilled when we heard that we had won. The prize was a hamper of Christmas goodies from one of the best shops in London, including a free-range turkey.

The turkey lasted days, even with Mac coming over

It would have been very un-Christmassy not to invite him in for a mince pie...

his ladder and hung them for us. I have no head for heights, and I wasn't about to let Kelly go up a ladder.

"We've entered the council competition," I told him more cordially. "The one for the most environmentally-friendly Christmas house."

"I know," said Mac sheepishly. "I saw your entry form. I have a confession to make – the competition was my idea. There's going to be a story in the local newspaper about the most wasteful house – that's mine – and the house that wins the competition. It's a way of getting the message across to people."

"Do you work for the council?" asked Kelly, who was quick on the uptake.

"Yes, I'm their environmental officer."

We fell about laughing in the kitchen. Daisy couldn't stand the noise and fled; she has sensitive ears.

to share our Christmas lunch and, later, cold turkey sandwiches. His lights never went on again. He was too embarrassed to switch them on, he said.

Even Daisy was delighted with our win. She adored giblets and was smuggled little bits of turkey under the table.

Daisy was half the reason why we won, apparently. A beautiful white cat sitting on snowballs in a white wheelbarrow was a picture not easily beaten.

A WORD FROM THE AUTHOR
"Daisy, my little tortoiseshell cat, was playing on a pile of bubble wrap one day, bursting the bubbles with her claws. It sounded just like softly falling snow. Heigh-ho, Christmas!"

Fancy That!

Christmas facts that make you go *"Wow!"*

Get a move on, Rudolph!

Santa would have to visit 822 homes a second, travelling at 650 miles a second, to deliver all the world's presents on Christmas Eve

■ **We use nearly 3,000 tons of tin foil to wrap our turkeys!**

■ It's estimated that 400,000 people get sick each year from eating tainted Christmas leftovers.

■ **If you received all of the gifts in The Twelve Days of Christmas, you would receive 364 presents!**

Eat an apple on Christmas Eve for good health the next year

■ **Only 45% of the world's population celebrate Christmas.**

■ The world's tallest Christmas tree, in a Washington shopping mall in 1950, was 221ft tall.

Eat a mince pie on each of the 12 days of Christmas to bring happiness in the year to come

According to a survey, 7 out of 10 dogs get Christmas gifts from their doting owners

■ **Santa's elves are the modernisation of the Nature Folk or Fae of the Pagan religions, and his reindeer are associated with the Horned God, the Pagan deity of nature.**

■ The movie *How the Grinch Stole Christmas* features 52,000 Christmas lights, 8200 Christmas ornaments, and nearly 2000 candy canes!

■ *A Christmas Carol* **was written by Charles Dickens in 1843 – it took him just six weeks!**

Christmas trees became popular in the UK from 1841, when Prince Albert erected a tree in Windsor Castle following a German tradition.

Festive
Teatime Treat

Snowflake Sprinkle

Silver Sparkle

Pipe pale blue buttercream thickly on top of plain cupcakes. Decorate with a large fondant icing snowflake, mini snowflakes and edible silver balls.

Festive Fairy

Pipe pink buttercream in a swirl on top of pink cupcakes and decorate with mini marshmallows and edible pearls. Top with a wired sugar star "wand".

Perfectly Pink

Deep Fill Cupcakes

Preparation time: 30mins plus cooling
Cooking time: 25mins
Makes 9 deep cupcakes

Ingredients

- 150g unsalted butter or margarine, softened
- 150g caster sugar
- 3 medium eggs
- 1tsp vanilla extract
- 200g self-raising flour

● Preheat the oven to 190°C, Fan Oven 170°C, Gas Mark 5. Line 9 muffin tins with muffin cases of your choice. Beat together the butter or margarine with the sugar until pale, soft and creamy.

Twinkly Tree

Minty Marvel

Santa's Hat!

Ho! Ho! Ho!

Fill red-coloured cupcakes with strawberry jam. Pipe red buttercream in a spiral on top of each cake. Decorate with mini marshmallows.

Pipe green buttercream, flavoured with peppermint essence, in a spiral on a chocolate cupcake. Decorate with silver balls and other sprinkles.

● Whisk in the eggs and vanilla extract until well blended. Sieve over the flour and mix together.

● Divide the mixture between the cake cases, filling them quite full. Smooth over the tops and bake in the oven for about 25mins, until risen and firm to the touch. Transfer to a wire rack to cool.

For Buttercream Icing

Beat 150g unsalted butter until smooth. Sieve in 225g icing sugar, beating well. Add colouring and mix well to make a smooth icing.

To Fill A Cup Cake

Scoop out a little cooked sponge and add your filling. Sit the scooped out sponge back on top and decorate.

One White Christmas

Even amidst a blizzard and the frustration of disrupted plans, goodwill and festive spirit can shine through...

By Donald Lightwood

he Christmas decorations in the village primary school sparkled with colour and the snow outside added the perfect seasonal touch.

However John Murdoch, the head teacher, was not a happy man. It was the afternoon of Christmas Eve and instead of being at home with his family, he had to open up the school to provide emergency accommodation.

Blizzard conditions had blocked the main road, trapping people in their vehicles. Volunteers from the village were

"It was my fault," she said. "Dad was right. We never should have set out. Gran would have understood if we'd phoned."

"It'll be the first Christmas we haven't all been together," mourned Jane.

"We're safe, that's the main thing."

"What will we do now?" asked Danny.

"Have something to eat, and then try and get some sleep."

"It's only six o'clock," his son protested.

As usual Jane had her mobile in her hand. "Text from Liz: *av a A P Xmas*."

"It's all right for her," grumbled Danny. "At home with a proper bed."

"There's a library corner, look." Tom pointed. "You could find yourself a book."

"I thought it would be dodgy, but I never expected anything like this"

bringing in families from the freezing cold. John was doing his best to settle the disgruntled travellers in the school hall.

Tom Davies and his family were grateful for their rescue.

"Think! We could have frozen to death," said Danny, Tom's twelve-year-old son. Nobody accused him of exaggerating.

"I prayed," admitted his fourteen-year-old sister. Her mother, Brenda, put her arm round her.

Danny and Jane tiptoed through the groups sitting on the floor.

"I'm sorry, Tom," Brenda murmured.

"I know. I thought it would be dodgy, but I never expected anything like this."

"I'll never hope for a white Christmas again as long as I live. Oh, Tom, look..."

A young couple had arrived. Brenda cast a professional eye over the heavily pregnant woman. "Goodness, she's pretty far on. She can't sleep on the floor."

She went over to John Murdoch, who was looking extremely concerned. "I'm a nurse," she told him. "Maybe I can help."

"Thank goodness," he said, relieved.

"We need a bed and privacy for this lady if possible."

"The medical room?" said John.

"Perfect," Brenda replied. "Everyone will be jealous of you," she told the young woman with a smile.

"We were on the way to the hospital,"

explained her husband.

"I don't think it'll be long," said his wife.

"Everything will be fine," soothed Brenda, taking the woman's hands. "Come on, let's get you settled down."

"Where's Mum?" Jane asked her father. She glanced around anxiously, looking for Brenda.

"Looking after an expectant mother," **Continued overleaf...**

Tom informed her. "It looks like the baby might arrive any time."

"Wow! I must text Liz."

"Imagine, spending Christmas in a school," said Danny. "Ugh."

"It'll be something to tell your children," remarked Tom.

"I'm not going to have kids," said Jane.

"And there was me looking forward to being a grandad," teased Tom.

"*He* can have the kids," said Jane, pointing at Danny.

"No way. Kids are rubbish."

"You should know," returned his sister.

A man came and stood beside them. "Mind if I join you?" he asked Tom.

"Be my guest. Pull up an armchair."

The man grinned and sat on the floor.

"Me?" the girl cried. "Is she going to have her baby?"

"It's likely."

"But I don't know anything about having babies."

"I can't think of a better way to find out," said Brenda briskly. "Come along."

A little while later John Murdoch and a policewoman came into the hall. John got everyone's attention and spoke. "Ladies and gentlemen, I'd like to introduce the officer responsible for co-ordinating your rescue; Sergeant Mowat."

She stepped forward. "First of all let me say how glad I am to see you all safe and to thank Mr Murdoch for putting the school at our disposal. I also have to tell

The people in the hall were not to hear the final carol as a sudden cry rang out

"It's the wife," he said, pulling a face. "According to her, this is all my fault. I should've known the snow would be bad."

"We were all caught out," said Tom.

"That's what I told her. The road was passable with care, the forecast said. She said I've spoilt the family's Christmas."

Jane looked at Danny. "We heard a man saying that to his wife."

"There's lots of people arguing," observed Danny.

He was right. The groups dotted around the hall were anything but happy.

"I think they should remember how lucky we are," Jane said. "We could have frozen to death."

Tom surveyed the crowded hall and nodded. "It's funny how it always seems so much worse when things go wrong at Christmastime."

Brenda appeared. "Jane, I need you."

you that I have just lost an argument. It was with the farmers and workers who rescued you from your vehicles. They did a fantastic job with their tractors, finding you and getting you out. However they would not come into the hall, I'm afraid. To me they are all heroes and they deserve the biggest thank you of all."

There was a tremendous burst of heartfelt applause as people were reminded of what really mattered. Indeed, the wife of the downcast man who had joined Tom came over to take his hand and lead him back to their children.

"Father Christmas will have a job finding us," said Danny wryly. "Did you eat the mince pie we used to leave for him?"

"Mum put it back in the tin and we crept upstairs with your presents."

"I knew it must be you. We don't have a chimney."

Tom nodded. "Central heating has robbed Christmas of some of its magic."

The mood in the hall had changed. There was more friendly chatter, as people spoke to strangers and compared experiences. There was even laughter. Danny teamed up with some teenagers and they went outside to make a

snowman. A lorry driver spoke to Tom.

"I've never known anything like this," he said. "They say it's global warming. How do they work that out? The snow was over our knees."

At that point John and the pub landlady came in with a tureen of soup and a tray of mince pies. They were warmly welcomed. The pies were freshly baked and the atmosphere began to feel more like a party than an emergency.

"Will you look at them!" someone cried. The kids outside were having a snowball fight.

"Do them good," commented the lorry driver. "Better for them than sitting here glued to their mobiles."

As the evening wore on it seemed quite natural that someone would sit down at the piano and play carols. Within moments there was singing. More and more joined in and it sounded as though the school was hosting a visiting choir.

For John Murdoch it was a unique experience, seeing his school transformed. His worries slid away and he found to his surprise he was enjoying himself. When the singing ended, he had an idea. It was almost midnight and he switched on the television at the end of the hall.

A watchnight service was being shown. After their own singing, people watched quietly, enjoying the glorious music from some cathedral. They listened to the words of the Christmas story as the Gospel was read out. Peace and goodwill descended on the hall.

The congregation rose for their final carol – but the viewers in the hall were not to hear it. What they did hear was the cry of a newborn baby.

A brief, shocked silence was followed by a great cheer. People hugged and kissed each other, danced and whooped like an American TV audience. More cries came. There was no doubt: a baby had been born on Christmas Day.

Jane came rushing into the hall. Her look of excitement and astonishment caused a few laughs. She steadied herself and then made her announcement.

"It's a girl!" she told them, and reached for her phone to text Liz.

A WORD FROM THE AUTHOR

"Having had two Christmas holidays ruined by the weather, this story was inevitable. Written with crossed fingers."

Baby Love

Christmas is a time for family and for happiness, but also a time to look back and be grateful for the way things are

By Elaine Chong

"Turkey's a versatile bird," Mike says. "A bit like you, Sheila," he adds with a chuckle and he wipes his hands on my apron then hangs it back on its hook behind the kitchen door.

I'm still drying up. It's our evening ritual after dinner.

Chrissie and Daniel are waiting for him in the hallway. He's taking them down the road to the club for the evening, because he knows I like to have this time on my own since Mum died.

It's the night before Christmas, and the turkey is sitting in a roasting pan on the side ready to be stuffed.

My mum always opened a box of the dried stuff and a plastic covered roll of pale, pink sausage meat. She mixed it together with her hands and filled the inside of the turkey till it looked like an over-inflated rugby ball.

These days we follow celebrity chef recipes. I have red onions, fresh fruit and what the packet describes as "aromatic herbs", waiting in a bowl in the fridge.

Mum would laugh if she could see me.

"Cooking is something you *do*, Sheila," she used to say to me with a laugh, "not

something you read about in a book."

I'm going to peel the potatoes and carrots next. Mike likes brussel sprouts and mashed swede with lots of butter and pepper. Chrissie wants purple sprouting broccoli and sugarsnap peas.

How times change. Mum always cooked cabbage with a roast no matter what day of the week it was.

Through the kitchen window I can see the first sign of snow. It's just a dusting of white on the pavement and will probably be nothing more than a memory by morning. But it feels like Christmas. The presents are wrapped under the tree, and the house is brightly decorated with coloured lights, even on the outside! Picture perfect, that's how it all looks.

Through the kitchen window I see the first sign of snow. It feels like Christmas

I start to peel the potatoes but when I look up, the face reflected back at me in the kitchen window is filled with sadness. I see the tears running down my cheeks before I feel them.

"Stop that now," I tell myself crossly, but I can't, no matter how hard I try.

Two months too early, that's what they said that Christmas Eve, when the ambulance came for us. So many years ago now, but it still feels like yesterday.

"You have to go in, love," Mike told me gently. "I'll follow on behind in the car

with your mother." He took my hands in his, lifted them to his mouth and kissed the tips of my fingers. "It'll be fine," he said, and drew me out of the house.

The grass on the front lawn was covered in a hard frost. Under the lights it looked like a carpet of diamonds. Even the air was crystal clear. I breathed it in and felt the cold seep into my veins.

In the ambulance the pain came and went in ever-quickening waves.

When we reached the hospital, I was quickly wheeled away, and Mum went off in search of a cup of sweet tea. Mike was left to pace the empty, echoing corridors. Stainless steel and bright, white lights, those were the last things my brain registered before I slipped into sleep.

I can't remember if it was the night air

Continued overleaf…

Continued from previous page

or the sound of singing that woke me. Everybody laughs when I tell the story now, but I thought I'd died. All around me the air was damp and cold, and I could hear distant voices singing, "Gloria, Hosanna in Excelsis."

I felt as if I was floating on a cloud. Slowly I opened my eyes. At first it was dark and then suddenly there was a blinding flash, and a voice said, "Somebody shut that window!"

As my eyes adjusted to the light, Mum's beaming face smiled down at me.

"It's a girl, Sheila," she whispered. "And she's a beauty."

She cradled a bundle of white blanket and nestled inside it was a tiny, sleeping baby. She reached down and slipped her

"That's what mums are for, my love," she whispered and pulled me into her arms.

All at once I feel a cold blast of air and a door slams. Chrissie tiptoes into the kitchen behind me but I can see her face reflected in the window. She looks happy,

"That's what mums are for, love," she whispered and pulled me into her arms

gently into the crook of my arm.

"She's so small," I said in a quiet voice.

"She's a fighter," Mum said proudly. "Just like you, my love."

I looked down at the precious bundle in my arms. She was beautiful, but so very small and fragile. I knew at once that I could never do this on my own and my eyes filled with tears.

Mum carefully lifted her from my arms and placed her back into the crib at the end of the bed, then she came to sit beside me. She pushed a damp strand of hair from my forehead and traced her fingers over my tear-stained cheeks.

"Sheila," she told me gently, "I know you're scared. I know it wasn't supposed to be like this, but you're not on your own. I'll always be here for you." She bent down and kissed the top of my head.

glowing, and when she hugs me tightly, we both feel the baby kick, and we laugh.

"Had a nice birthday?" I ask her.

"Lovely," she says. "You always make this a special day for me. I don't know what I'd do without you, Mum. You're always there for me," she says and her voice quivers with emotion.

I turn around and draw her into my arms. "That's what mums are for," I tell her, and know the night before Christmas will never be filled with sadness again.

A WORD FROM THE AUTHOR

"It's often mothers and daughters who share the joyful expectation of a birth, and the sadness of missing those they love."

Make Time For

My Weekly

- It's packed with top relaxing **fiction**
- Practical **health** advice
- **Celebrity** news and **real life** stories
- Super **recipes** for every occasion

Great Value

ON SALE EVERY TUESDAY

PLUS Your Photos, Fashion and Beauty, Diet and Wellbeing, Fascinating Facts, Puzzles & Lots More

No 1 FOR FICTION